CW00393646

Twenty
Walks Around
RUGBY

by Rugby Ramblers
edited by John Roberts

```
*********************************
```
WALKWAYS
J S Roberts
8 Hillside Close, Bartley Green
Birmingham B32 4LT
```
*********************************
```

Twenty
Walks around Rugby

by Rugby Ramblers
edited by John Roberts

© Rugby Ramblers Association
and John Roberts 1994

ISBN 0 947708 30 8

First Published 1994

WALKWAYS

DaywalkS Footpath Networks

Networks of linked paths from which you can make your own circular walks.

Cannock Chase (£4.20)
Vale of Llangollen (£4.20)
Wyre Forest (£4.20)

Strolls & Walks

From each of about twenty places there is a stroll of a mile of so and a walk of 4 to 6 miles.

Strolls & Walks from Picnic Places (Midlands) (£3.95)
Strolls & walks from Cotswold Villages (£5.50)
Strolls & Walks from Midland Villages (out 1995)

Long Distance Routes

Step by step guides in both directions which often connect with each other and Long Distance Footpaths. (A2 sheets folded to A5 (£1.35), but Heart of England Way is a book (£4.55)

Llangollen to Bala   Bala to Snowdon
Birmingham to Ludlow   Ludlow to Rhayader
Rhayader to Aberystwyth
Birmingham to Church Stretton
Heart of England Way

8 Hillside Close, Bartley Green, Birmingham
B32 4LT   021 550 3158

Publishers Note
& Standing Offer

This book exists because Kelvin Hunt of Hunt's Bookshop in Rugby mentioned that the local Group of the Ramblers Association wanted to bring out a book of walks. I said that if I could help they should contact me; I knew some of the Group through my involvement with Warwickshire Area RA.

When we met to discuss the project I was able to offer a range of services. The Group could just hand me what they had written and I would arrange for printing, or I could edit their work, or I could do further research and supplement it, or I could walk the paths and rewrite the directions, etc etc. In the event they sent me their walk descriptions and decided that I should follow all the paths and provide a new text. I was able to do this and extend the comment and information, supply photos and present them with a full draft of an expanded manuscript written from a fresh viewpoint. My usual WALKWAYS format and approach suited the Group, though they could have had any other they wished. At all times the Group had the final say on the wording, but actually changed very little of what I wrote. It was highly enjoyable, especially the Rugby Town Walk, and I hope to repeat the experience elsewhere.

Here then, is a standing offer to any RA Group in England or Wales who want to publish their own book of local walks. I will provide any level of service you choose, from simply arranging the printing through to walking your paths and (if you wish) writing your book from scratch. The financial arrangements are attractive and not affected by how much work I do.

John Roberts
WALKWAYS

Meet Rugby Ramblers

The Rugby Group of the Ramblers Association (or Rugby Ramblers) was formed over 25 years ago to encourage use of local footpaths and organise walks for members.

We offer nearly 100 walks a year including morning and summer evening walks of between 4 and 7 miles and full day excursions of 10 to 12 miles. Occasionally we have outings of 22 or 26 miles. There are walks every Sunday and some midweek. Rugby's central position allows us to reach many beautiful places - the Cotswolds, The Welsh Borders and the Peak District. We have some weekend trips to the lake District, Yorkshire Dales and Snowdonia.

Our other important job is looking after the local footpath network. We report obstructions to the County Council and study diversion proposals or other developments which might affect paths. There are about 301 miles of footpaths and bridleways in the 40 Parishes within our area and we have just completed a full survey. Broken down stiles, blockages and the need for waymarking were all noted and sent to the County Council.

To promote our local paths we published our first book of walks in 1978, researched and described by members. A revised edition followed in 1982. Since then many points in the directions have changed and some of the old routes have lost their appeal due to building or modern arable farming. In this book we present the best of the old walks, thoroughly updated, and some new ones.

The Group researched the walks and drafted directions, adding notes and comments. John Roberts then followed each route, supplemented the information, took photographs and edited the directions into the format used in his other books.

Our thanks to Fred Clapham, a past Secretary, whose energy and enthusiasm made the first edition possible. Thanks to John Roberts, for updating, restyling and publishing the book. Thanks to Ken Banks, our past Chairman, who kept alive the idea of a third edition. Ken liased with John and with the help of our Footpath Secretary, Stan Patrick, carried out the huge task of checking the text.

We hope that you will enjoy walking these routes and exploring areas of our local countryside which you can only see on foot. It has much to offer at all seasons of the year. Help us preserve our heritage of footpaths for the next generation by going out to walk them now. The more they are used the easier they will be to follow.

Lastly - if you would like company, come and join us. The Group offers a warm welcome. For a copy of the programme and membership details contact - Mrs Fran Debonnaire, 3 Montgomery Drive, Rugby CV22 7EA - 0788 812213.

Graham Bevan
Chairman
November 1994

Contents

Rugby & District

With each walk you will find descriptions of the villages,
canals, railways, rivers and churches as you meet them. Here
we can draw together some of the main themes.

Rugby has been accused of having no heart or centre. It may
have no especially outstanding architecture, but our Town
Walk shows that there are very interesting and attractive
buildings, and Rugby has a pleasant, busy, small town
character. It also has some very distinct claims to fame.

Rugby means the great public school founded in 1567 by a
bequest from Lawrence Sheriff, a local tradesman. Rugby
means a game of football developed from an incident in 1823
when a boy at Rugby School picked up the ball and ran with
it. To architects Rugby means a feast of the highly coloured
Victorian work of William Butterfield who built important
parts of the School. To railway enthusiasts Rugby was and
remains one of the most important railway junctions in the
country. Electrical engineers see Rugby as the source of
GEC's monstrous motors and generators, snailing down the
roads on low loaders. They also make more portable items
including gears and electronic equipment. To the radio
engineer Rugby is the crop of spikey, cable festooned masts
sprouting near Hillmorton. And for poetry lovers Rugby was
the home of Rupert Brooke.

The town sits on a low ridge of which the highest part is
near the dramatic Ashlawn Water Tower at 120 metres. A
youthful River Avon flows east to west across the north side
at about 83 metres, to the south the Rainsbrook flows much
the same way at 90 metres. These are no great rises or falls
but enough to add some attractive variety to the area.

The countryside around the town is not, therefore, dramatic
landscape, rather, gently rolling green fields which draw

their charm from hedgerows and trees. This is the state of things also to the north and west, towards Lutterworth and Coventry. But when you move south-west, south and to the east you meet vigorous contours which ripple and climb - in fact the northern fringe of the Northamptonshire Uplands. In simple terms then, Rugby sits on the edge of a plain which gives way to rolling hills.

This general picture of the landscape is reflected in these walks. Those near Rugby, from villages such as Clifton upon Dunsmore and Newbold on Avon and from the suburbs of Hillmorton and Bilton, explore the intimacies of a level countryside - mills, canals, old tracks and churches, with an occasional hill. But the more distant walks, such as Barby, Honey Hill and West Haddon have shapely hills and grassy slopes with long views.

The stone buildings also reflect the landscape, particularly the churches. They are generally built from a mixture of soft red sandstone, a brown ironstone and sometimes a blue, clayey looking stone called Blue Lias. None of them wears very well, so the churches look rather gaunt and wasted, but they show what local masons had to work with. The ironstone is from Northants, part of the belt of Jurassic limestone which reaches from the Cotswolds to the Yorkshire Wolds. The Lias comes from the clay plain to the north and west in which the sandstone occurs as outcrops.

Come out with us and enjoy our local countryside. You will meet the Oxford Canal which wanders all over the place and the Grand Union which runs in straight lines. There are the broad cuttings and blue brick arches of the Great Central Railway, that latecomer to the main system with ambitions to reach France via Rugby through a Channel Tunnel, but which ended at Marylebone. Look out for the Ashlawn Water Tower, Thurlaston and Barby mills, the Hillmorton Masts and the Rainsbrook which divides Warwickshire from Northants. We can even find something nice to say about the M45.

Light rain over the Avon at Little Lawford

The Country Code

* Enjoy the countryside and respect its life and work
* Guard against all risk of fire
* Fasten all gates
* Keep your dogs under close control
* Keep to public paths across farmland
* Use gates and stiles to cross fences, hedges and walls
* Leave livestock, crops and machinery alone
* Take your litter home
* Help to keep water clean
* Protect wildlife, plants and trees
* Take special care on country roads
* Make no unecessary noise

Boots and Clothes and things

These walks are all modest affairs and you do not need to go equipped for mountaineering. There are many books that offer sound advice on boots, clothing and equipment if you want to take up walking as a pastime.

This part of the Midlands can be very muddy in wet weather. Walking boots are best, but for short walks wellies will do fine if you find them comfortable. Trainers are excellent in dry weather. You do not necessarily need two pairs of socks but a good thickness of woolly padding is a great comfort. The traditional grey, rough wool rag sock is hardwearing and reasonably thick, but that is about all. Try loop pile socks. It will usually be sensible to take a hat and waterproof.

Rights of Way & Obstructions

These walks are all on public Rights of Way or in places where the public is permitted to walk. They may be Footpaths, Bridleways or Byways (usually green lanes or tracks) with some stretches of ordinary road. Your rights as pedestrian are the same on all, you are entitled to follow the track or cross the land. The fact that it is "private" (most land is) is quite irrelevant.

Occupiers of land are legally obliged not to obstruct paths, it is an offence, but sometimes they do. Paths should not be ploughed up nor have crops growing over them, nor should you meet barbed wire fences. You are entitled to cross or remove any such obstacles doing as little damage as you reasonably can. You may diverge to pass the obstacle so long as you go no further than necessary and do not enter someone else's land.

These notes appear in all WALKWAYS books but it is not likely that you will meet real problems on these walks. If you do please write to our Footpath Secretary or phone messages through the publisher.

Amendment Service

The countryside changes all the time. You could meet new tracks, stiles and barns; hedges vanish and paths may be diverted. To keep directions as up to date as possible WALKWAYS issues amendment slips.

IF you write to tell us of any changes or problems that you meet, stating route and paragraph number, we will refund your postage.

IF you send a stamped addressed envelope with a note of what publication(s) you have, we will send you up to date amendment slips. (Phone enquiries welcome - 021 550 3158)

Using the Directions

You will see that the Directions are quite separate from the description and comment, very terse and set in short, narrow, numbered paragraphs in a clear and open typeface. These and less obvious features have been adopted for WALKWAYS books after much experience and thought. The aim is to give you information in easily located and remembered blocks of convenient a size, bearing in mind that you will be reading them on the move.

Distances in YARDS or MILES are to give you a rough idea how far to walk. You do not have to try and measure.

Distance in PACES are there to be counted out, if you need to. Paces vary but you can allow for being very tall or short. The reason for all this is that people carry a pace with them but not usually a measuring tape, and very few of us have got a clue what 200 yards looks like.

The maps are sketches to an approximate scale of 2ins/1mile. They are designed to confirm where you are rather than for route finding. The meanings of the symbols are mainly obvious but we show a few of them below. The numbers of selected paragraphs from the route descriptions appear on the maps. The big black arrow on each map points north.

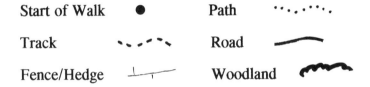

For each walk we note the relevant Ordnance Survey maps. In fact, you should manage very well with the directions and sketch maps, but a general map of the area is neccessary to find starting points.

The Ordnance Survey Landranger series (1.25 inches/mile; 2 cms/km) are the most convenient to carry for general interest. You would need three sheets, 140, 151 and 152.

The more detailed Pathfinder sheets (2.5 inches/mile; 4 cms/km) are for people really addicted to maps. They will need five sheets, SP46/56, 47/57/, 48/58, 66/76 and 67/77.

List of Walks

Second and third distances are of alternative walks

General Map

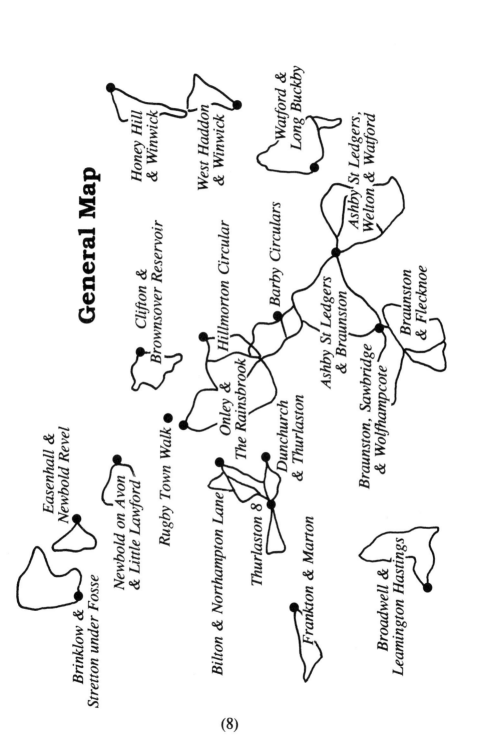

Honey Hill & Winwick

West Haddon & Winwick

Watford & Long Buckby

Ashby St Ledgers, Welton, & Watford

Clifton & Brownsover Reservoir

Hillmorton Circular

Barby Circulars

Braunston & Flecknoe

Easenhall & Newbold Revel

Onley & The Rainsbrook

Ashby St Ledgers & Braunston

Newbold on Avon & Little Lawford

Rugby Town Walk

Dunchurch & Thurlaston

Braunston, Sawbridge & Wolfhampcote

Bilton & Northampton Lane

Brinklow & Stretton under Fosse

Thurlaston 8

Frankton & Marton

Broadwell & Leamington Hastings

(8)

Rugby Town Walk

PARK/START

Park in one of the town centre car parks and buy a ticket for at least two hours. This is a short walk but there are lots of pauses. Start from the Clock Tower.

Visit the Tourist Information Centre in the Library for more information on some of the buildings.

(1) Stand near the clock and look about.

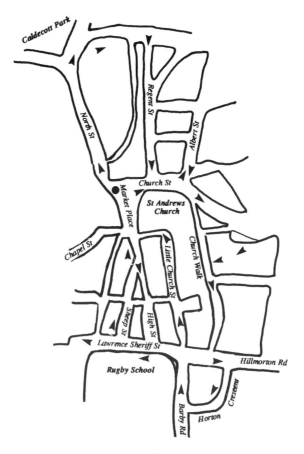

The *Clock Tower* was built in 1887 for Queen Victoria's
Golden Jubilee. The Darley Dale stone structure has ginger
ironstone panels on a granite base. The *Crown Hotel*
looks old but dates from 1903 and the timber work is just
decorative. *Prudential Chambers* are mid 19th century with
balustraded parapet, Italianate roof, wrought iron balcony
rails, and the emphatic first floor windows with heavy broken
pediment arches. *The Rugby Centre* has a modern interior
behind a 19th century facade with cheery little Ionic columns
supporting warm brickwork. Next door the TSB has tapered
Ionic pilasters which seem huge pale imitations. Beyond
is the *Rayner Building,* a grotesque from 1893 with madly
proportioned windows, bows, dormers and a tiddly widdly
spire.

(2) From the clock walk into Church Street.

On your left the *curved row of shops* built in the 1960's
replaced Webbs, an 18th century baroque house, and the
Sheriffe Alms Houses of 1567.

St Andrew's Church has a 13th century tower at one end
which is dwarfed by Butterfield's 19th century gothic one
at the other, and hence two peals of bells. The rest of the
structure was originally 14th and 15th century but again,
Butterfield swamped it with his nave. The interior is huge
and high and terribly gothic, the chancel a riot of intense
embellishment with a complicated east window, while the
nave has two tone pillars in brown and cream sandstone.
No one could accuse Butterfield of restraint.

Opposite the church is a *block of three banks,* and a house.
Lloyds was built in 1904 in extravagant French renaissance
style; a bit flip for a bank. The Midland is poker faced
and seems to be watching you. These two should envy the
warm red brick and generous windows of the Royal Bank of
Scotland (1867), suggesting genial and meticulous care of
your money. The yellow brick house between the banks has
a three storey bow window, plain but beautifully done.

(3) Cross the road now for a look down Albert Street.

Note the comfortable low slung *corner building* with
the Italianate roof. The style has terrific presence and
poise, and while different from its neighbours it does not
clash. Further on are the classical Victorian *Conservative
Association* and the *Post Office*. The latter was built in
1983 and is just like its neighbour, but it has no presence.
Opposite, the *Estate Office* has a corner door in a smooth
stone facade from the 1920's. There are art nouveau twiddles
round doors, baroque flourishes over windows and the
wreath on the corner looks like a huge, ripe, door knocker.

(4) Return to Church Street and on to the Squirrel Inn.

On the right the tophatted gent and black facia at *Lloyds*
look fittingly gloomy. The *Squirrel Inn* was made from three
cottages dating from between 1775 and 1820. Opposite is *The
Plaisance* where there was once a horse pool and ducking
stool. Now there are square loos, square flower beds, square
flags in square patterns and square iron tree cages on square
grills, with round trees.

(5) Enter St Andrew's Gardens and bear right.

The *Gardens* were the old parish churchyard on part of which
Holy Trinity Church was built in 1852 and demolished in the
1970's. On the left as you leave is the *Wratislaw Memorial*.
This local family came from Bohemia and were prominent in
Rugby for nearly two hundred years.

(6) Enter Church Walk and go left to Hillmorton Road.

On the left, *Arnold Villas,* which are mid 19th century have
romantic little upper windows and discreet heraldry. Yellow
and honey brick is more often seen in southern England, but
this came from a local clay which ran out in 1855. Look for
further examples as we go on. At the end of Church Walk on
the left is the house where the poet *Rupert Brooke* was born
in 1887. He and his father were masters at Rugby School.

(7) Go left up to Horton Crescent on the right.

On the left is a fine *yellow brick terrace* with a gorgeous filigree wrought iron balcony. Next door No.17 is in Victorian Tuscan style with an invisibly modest tower, a great chunky upper roof and hexagonal lower one; a lot of romanticness packed into a small space.

(8) Turn right down Horton Crescent, bearing right at the island and on to Barby Road.

On the right corner is *Horton House,* a big handsome Butterfield, and others follow. After the island you can see on the left another *School Building* by Butterfield. The staircase tower links several radiating wings. The narrow, round headed windows are more lighthouse than church, but the roof looks like a dunce's cap.

(9) Turn right down Barby Road to the junction.

On the left the grassy mound under the trees is *The Island.* This ancient tumulus could once be seen from similar mounds in nearby villages. In 1797 it was the scene of the last stand in the great School Rebellion. Disaffected boys had broken shop windows and blown open the door to the Headmaster's study with gunnpowder. Finally the Yeomanry turned out and the boys retreated to the Island, which was surrounded by a moat 12 feet wide and 5 deep. The Magistrates read the Riot Act, and encircled by the Army and local farmers with horse whips, the boys surrendered.

The *statue* on the right is of Thomas Hughes who did time at Rugby School between 1834 and 1842 and wrote the near autobiographical *Tom Brown's Schooldays.* He seems to be asking which boy shot off the cowboy hat which lies on the ground. (Why no statue of George Macdonald Frazer who has more recently chronicled the life of Tom Brown's tormentor, Flashman?)

The *gates* to the School playing fields on the left were erected in 1967 to mark 400 years of Rugby School. They are plain and pleasing but we wonder what Butterfield might have turned out. On the wall inside is a plaque commemorating the exploit of William Webb Ellis in 1823 who, "took the ball in his arms and ran with it, thus originating the distinctive feature of the Rugby Game".

On the right at the road junction is the *Temple Speech Room* of 1909 used for School assemblies and concerts. The green dome is magnificent, a sort of imperial sou-wester.

(10) Cross the road junction and walk down Little Church Street opposite, to its end.

On the left corner is the *New Big School* of 1885, you can guess the architect. It is now the School's theatre. The first building on the left houses the Rugby School Museum. At the end on the left is a simple Victorian *corner house* with a chamfered front in first class brickwork.

(11) At the junction with Market Place, cross into the start of Chapel Street.

On the left is a tiny *half timbered* building said to be over 600 years old and the oldest in Rugby. This was the butchers shop where Tom Brown came for a steak for his black eye after his fight with "Slogger" Williams.

(12) Return to Market Place and take the left fork down High Street to its end.

Three buildings on the corner of this junction have curved windows, and this may be the only Macdonald's in the world with a coat of arms. Most of the shop fronts are familiar, enough but look at the buildings above. There is the squarely classical *Briggs* building and dear old *Burton's* in its Tailors Assyrian style. The grand *Marks & Spencer* housed the Council Offices from 1900 to 1936. *Woolworths* is typical 1950's concrete slab with coloured tiles. At the end on the right is *Terra Cotta* arcaded, tiered, knobled and twiddled.

At the end of High Street you see part of *Rugby School.*
To the left are sober yellow/grey brick buildings by Henry
Hakewill from the early 1800's. The battlemented and towered
Headmaster's House curiously resembles some Scottish railway
stations. The big wooden *doors* are the main School entrance.
The more flamboyant block on the right is Butterfield again,
the polychrome brick continues round the corner and has been
called "a controlled riot".

> **(13) Turn right, cross the end of Sheep Street and Drury
> Lane into St Matthews Street.**

On the right is *James Gilbert's* shop and Rugby Football
Museum. They made the first oval balls and and still produce
match balls by hand. At the end on the right is the *Library,*
a very plain and humble public structure set beside Butterfield's fireworks behind you. Here also is the *Percival
Guildhouse,* an adult education centre. Opposite is the
Royal Wedding Clock, now a sad memorial.

> **(14) Turn back to see the school frontage and two
> chapels, then cross Drury Lane to go left down
> Sheep Street.**

The *Three Horse Shoes* has been an inn since 1728. It was a
meeting place for Rugby tradesmen who spent an evening each
week in the so called Horse Shoe Parliament discussing the
town's affairs. The frontage is typical early 18th century,
though restrained to the point of gauntness. The Victorian
front of the *Bull Hotel* is crowded with broad windows.

> **(15) Continue to Market Place and ahead down North
> Street to the roundabout.**

North Street has no buildings of great interest. At the end
is the *Gala Cinema* (formerly Granada), which proclaims its
new its vocation as Bingo Club five times across the canopy.
Perhaps some of these dull, monumental, 1930's cinemas ought
to be preserved. Across the road is the *Town Hall* of 1961.
The wings are quite anonymous and the high rigid central

columns slightly nasty. Next is *Caldecott Park* opened in 1904.

> **(16) Go right to cross the open area of trees and grass (Chestnut Field) to join the road, follow it a few yards, then walk up Regent Street right.**

On your left are *Jubilee Gardens,* once the site of the Baths, and a bit earlier of a pre Roman British fort. Go and see the statue of *Rupert Brooke.*

Further along to the right the red brick *Baptist Church* is in the Perpendicular style, except for the tapered tower which has a rollicking open-work iron spire. Past the church on the left is Henry Street. Here is a mighty *three gabled shop* with bowed upper windows which ought to be a forceful commercial presence, but is now empty. The single barn-like gable and bold arched entrance is the *Rugby Theatre.* It is owned and run by a voluntary group who at the time of our visit were promoting "Who Goes Bare - the hilarious farce." We hope that it cheers up the gloomy *Central Hall* opposite, its arches drooping like a depressed railway tunnel.

Walking on along Regent Street, notice the *continuous plate glass windows* of the frontage on the left, topped by two totally frivolous Dutch gables. The whole of this varied street was developed between 1900 and 1910 by the Rugby Building Society with a miscellany of styles and features. We have brickwork, rendering, timber framing, plaster, ironstone and the windows have bays, bows, oriels and some wrought iron balconies.

> **(17) At the end of Regent Street you are in Church Street. Go right and back to the Town Clock.**

Braunston Marina

Plaster and thatch at Barby

(16)

Ashby St Ledgers
& Braunston

WHERE?
Map reference SP 568682. Ashby is about 7 miles south-east
of Rugby on the A361 Kilsby - Daventry road.

PARK/START
Park on the main village street near the Olde Coach House
Inn, and start from this pub.

HOW FAR?/FACILITIES
About 6.5 miles mainly on field paths, but there are some
bridleways so expect mud in wet weather. Pubs at the start
and Braunston.

You can combine this walk with some other Braunston routes,
Braunston & Flecknoe or Braunston, Wolfhampcote & Sawbridge.
This would give walks of; B & F - Route (A) 11.5 miles, Route
(B) 13 miles and B, W & S - 10.5 miles. Just switch from this
walk at Paragraph (4) and pick it up again later at Para (5).

MAPS
Landranger sheets 151 & 2, Pathfinder SP 46/56 (977).

ASHBY ST LEDGERS & DISTRICT
Ashby is a village of one sleepy street which feels
surprisingly remote and isolated. Some houses are in red
brick and tile, but the visitor is caught by the rich golden
brown stone. Approached from the main road, much of the
rural atmosphere is added by the dark and heavily thatched
cottages near the pub, though they were built only in 1908.

Like all places with names ending in "by", Ashby was a
Danish village. It appears in the Domesday Book, has an
Elizabethan manor house, and in a room over the Manor
gateway, William Catesby and friends probably hatched the
Gunpowder plot. Get the booklet from the church.

The church of St Leodegarius (Ledger) stands on the site of a Norman or earlier church. The present building is mainly from the 14th century, very mellow and worn. A Jacobean three decker central pulpit is simply carved under a proud canopy, there are traces of medieval wall paintings with a skeleton depicting the Black Death and a throbbingly colourful Victorian east window. But look longest at the breathtaking rood screen dating from about 1500. With the box pews between the screen and the nave, the chancel is almost a secret cave.

If the colour of the stone reminds you of iron, remember that the Northamptonshire town of Corby is not far away, and had one of the largest opencast ore mines in Europe. And if you are reminded of the Cotswolds, Ashby stands on the same great belt of Jurassic limestone which runs from Bath to the Yorkshire wolds. The colour of the stone seems to grow deeper to the north.

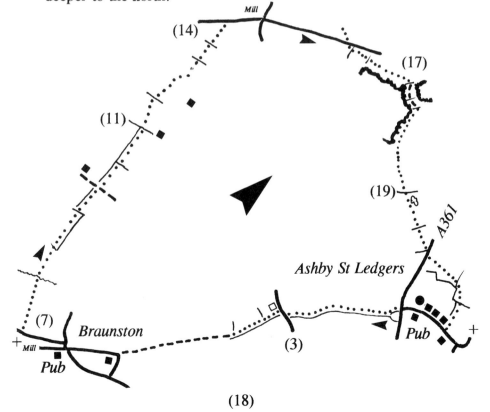

(18)

*

(1) Face Olde Coach House Inn & go R to A361.

(2) Take gate opposite & circle round trees L, to hedge. Go with hedge on your L, via 3 fields (appx .6 mile) to road.

(3) Go R appx 100yds & take 2nd (ie small) gate L by black shed. Go with hedge on your L, via small gates, to join track.

[Note the deep ridge and furrow in the first field, a survival of medieval farming which occurs in much of Warwickshire. We hope it is not raining so hard as to obscure views of this exuberantly rolling landscape with Braunston church and mill.]

(4) Follow appx .6 mile to road bend (Braunston). Go ahead .3 mile to Wheatsheaf Inn.

****
[To join Braunston walks, break off here.]
****

(5) Take road R (Barby) 50yds, then street L. Follow 400yds & take path R between Nos 52 & 54.

◄

(6) Follow path & short street to junction, then down The Countryside to bottom, & take gate/stile.

(7) Go ahead midfield to midhedge "gate". [No - we know it isn't, but it looks like one.] Cross plank bridge to field.

(8) Go up with hedge on your R, drawing away from it to take midhedge field end gate.

[Look back for a view of Braunston. On the skyline right of the church is a post Office tower. Quite soon you will see ahead some of the radio masts at Hillmorton.]

(9) Go with hedge on your L to stile & track. Take gate opposite. Make for L side of farm ahead & take gate.

(10) Cross field diagonally & take corner stile. Go with hedge on your L & take field end gate AHEAD.

[The name of Tiltup's Holt Farm on the right is striking as its location, on the sharp slope of Cleve's Hill.]

►

(11) Bear L with L hedge appx 50yds till it bends away L. NB trough ahead & lone tree up L. Go to tree & take stile.

(12) Bear L to 75yds L of R field corner, & take midhedge stile.

(13) Keep same line via stiles (thro new trees) to stile & road.

[The plastic Tully tubes are sprouting with oak, beech, wild cherry, holly and blackthorn.]

(14) Go R to cross roads.

[Here are three miserable looking objects, a topless, windowless mill, a spidery radio mast and an octopus legged water tower. This has nautical railings and what look like portholes.]

(15) Go ahead (Kilsby) .5 mile. Pass path sign & stile L & take stile R.

(16) Go L over field corner & take twin stiles. Go ahead midfield via gate, then with wood on your R to corner of wood & pine plantation.

(17) Take gate R & follow green track to take gate. Go with hedge on your R & take gate R.

(18) Go with fence on your R to its corner. Keep same line appx 500yds & take midhedge gate/stile.

(19) Bear L to pass fenced area (pond) on your L. Keep same line, via dip, & up to gate & A361.

(20) Take stile opposite. Bear R to pass 50yds R of projecting hedge corner. KEEP SAME LINE to 25yds L of field corner, & cross plank bridge & stile.

(21) Go with hedge on your R to corner, then pass midfield power pole to far bottom field corner.

(22) Cross stream & go up parallel with R fence. Take stile under cypress tree & follow path to road. Go R to start.

Ashby St Ledgers, Welton & Watford

WHERE?
Map reference SP 573681. Ashby is about 7 miles south-east
of Rugby off the A361 Kilsby - Daventry road.

PARK/START
Park near the church. Start from the junction with the lane
to Welton.

HOW FAR?/FACILITIES
Route (A) is 6.75 miles and Route (B) 4.25. Both are mainly
on fieldpaths with attractive canal walking in (A) and a
lane in (B). Not notably muddy. There are pubs at Ashby,
Welton and canalside at Watford.

MAPS
Landranger sheet 152, Pathfinder SP 46/56 (977) (and a corner
only on) 66/76 (957).

ASHBY ST LEDGERS, WELTON & THE CANAL.
Ashby St Ledgers is a charming village with great atmosphere.
We have commented further in the other walk which starts
here, Ashby St Ledgers & Braunston, but there are two main
features. The ironstone church of St Leodegarius has Norman,
possibly Viking, origins but the present building dates from
the 14th century. There is a worn and mellow quality of this
stone that powerfully suggests great age, long tradition and
deep tranquillity.

The other main feature of Ashby has strong conections with
religion but little tranquility. The Manor is by the church
and you will not miss the little white, timber framed room
over the gateway where in 1605, the Gunpowder Plot was
hatched. The Catesby family had lived at Ashby since 1375
but during the Protestant ascendancy of Elizabeth I's reign
members were imprisoned and fined. The Plot can be seen

as a desperate reaction by persecuted Roman Catholics. Get the leaflet on the village and its history from the church.

Welton has a handful of buildings from the last century and earlier, but most are modern. It is a harmonious straggling mixture with the White Horse pub and the ginger ironstone church of St Martin. Look out for the handsome lead water cistern dated 1673 and embellished with swags of fruit and heraldry.

Between Welton and Watford the walk follows the Grand Union Canal past Norton Junction. It is the longest, most complex canal in the UK and was one of the the most important. Norton is a surprise. Here is no great road connection, no range of factories or warehouses and no shops, but a lonely lock and a keeper's cottage dreaming in the fields.

Plotting at Ashby St Ledgers

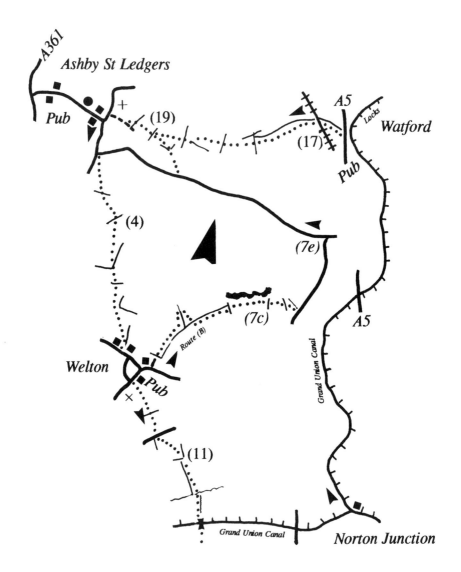

✳

Routes (A) & (B)

(1) From main street take lane to Welton 300yds to junction.

(2) Take gate/stile L on corner & go on a few paces up small rise. **NB skyline trees ahead have 2 big gaps.** Head for centre of R gap & take stile by POLE.

(3) Bear half L to pole in opposite hedge & cross plank bridge. **(As you descend NB HILLTOP trees & pole half R.)**

(4) Bear R to hilltop trees & pole, & take small gateway. Go with hedge on your R to its end.

(5) Bear L to pass bottom tree on your R & keep same line upfield, to pole on projecting hedge corner.

(6) Keep same line to far end of hedge L (becomes fence), & take stile & path to street.

(7) Go L & round R bend, to junction with Station Rd L.◄

◄ *Route (B)*

(7a) Take Station Rd L to end of houses. Go L & take end stile.

(7b) Go with hedge on your R & take field end gate. Go R, round field corner plus 50yds, & take stile R

(7c) Go with hedge on your L (via gate) to end of wood, & round field corner to take gate.

(7d) Head for farm & take black gate. Go R to gate & B4036.

(7e) Go L .5 mile & take lane L.

(7f) Follow appx .9 mile (past track L & under power lines, then 2nd track L & power lines) to DOUBLE steel gate R at end of small wood.

(7g) Take gate & go half L to big oak & projecting hedge corner. Cross fence & KEEP SAME LINE to take stile R of water trough.

NEXT Para (20) ▶

➤ Route (A)

(8) From junction with Station Rd, go AHEAD 80yds & opposite steel barrier R, take path L.

(9) Follow & take stile. Go with hedge on your L & take field bottom stile L, then with hedge on your R to road.

(10) Take stile opposite, cross field diagonally & take far corner stile.

(11) Bear R & take L of 2 corner gates. Go with hedge on your R & cross corner bridge.

(12) Follow hedged track, take gate & with hedge on your R, cross canal bridge & join towpath.

[The sign "Cows Please Shut Gate" says much for our Agricultural Colleges and the cows.]

(13) DON'T GO UNDER BRIDGE, follow canal .75 mile to canal junction. ◢

[The Grand Union glides and winds through a landscape of green folds, now on a bank, now in a shallow cutting, as the fields rise and fall.]

(14) Follow canal towards LEICESTER (crossing brick bridge & wooden bridge) appx 1.8 miles;
   - pass boat yard
   - under 2 bridges & A5
   - under railway
   - under bridge, pass pub
to pumphouse & locks.

(15) Go up to 2nd lock & take small bridge L. Go ahead & pass house on your L to A5.

(16) Go L 20 paces & take stile R. Bear R past projecting hedge corner & take steps over railway **(GREAT CARE)** & down to field.

(17) Go with hedge on your R appx .4 mile, to cross R corner bridge & stile.

(18) Keep same line to cross twin stiles & bridge to field. Go to far L field corner & take R of 2 stiles.

(19) Go with hedge on your L & take stile. Go ahead up to R of gate & water trough, & cross stile.

◥ Route (B) rejoins

(20) Head for church & take stile under poplars, then to L end of wall. Go R (via gates) to start. ●

Barby Circulars

WHERE?
Map reference SP 543703, a village about 3.5 miles south-east of Rugby, best approached from the B4429 Dunchurch - Hillmorton road.

PARK/START
Start from the church and park nearby.

HOW FAR?/FACILITIES
Route (A) 4.7 miles, Route (B) 3.6 miles. You walk mainly on dry fieldpaths and tracks, but a short bridleway near the start of both Routes can be damp and dirty after wet weather. There is a pub in Barby.

MAPS
Landranger sheet 140, Pathfinder SP 47/57 (956) & 46/56 (977).

BARBY AND THE WALK
Barby is a hilltop settlement with the tower of St Mary's church and the mill visible for miles. This walk takes you over some of the contours and there are fine views to the south and west. The village has mostly new houses, but near the church are a few long, low whitewashed cottages with trim little windows under thatched brows.

St Mary's is built of pink sandstone with patches of ginger and bright yellow ironstone. The base of the square tower has palings and a very old sign "Beware falling Masonry". Most of the old churches on these walks are in a similar state, if not actually dangerous, showing the problems of unsuitable local materials. Railways and canals made it possible to import better materials, but brought a loss of local harmony and charm.

This walk crosses the M45 and the Oxford Canal. We have talked about the canal in other walks, Hillmorton Circular and Newbold on Avon & Little Lawford. Few books of walks mention motorways except to say rude things, but perhaps something can be said for the M45. With the M1 it was our first, part of the London to Birmingham Motorway of the long forgotten Ernest ("Must Go") Marples. After it opened cavalcades of jolly old British cars puffed and boiled, shook, rattled and bonked, and often conked out after their first wheel wobbling experience of travelling at more than 30mph for half an hour without a rest. Of course, the gallant little M45 never reached Birmingham, or even Coventry, and has been superceded by the awesome, loathsome M6. Now it is our only snoozing Beeching branch motorway where the odd car is watched thoughtfully by brown cows.

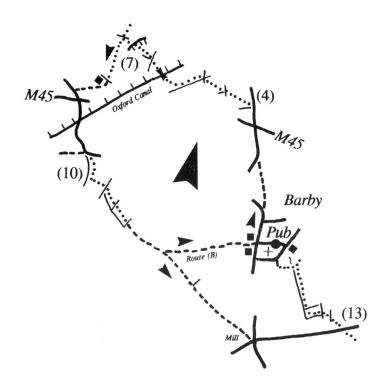

Routes (A) & (B)

(1) From church go to main road & turn R. Pass Arnold Arms & Ware Rd & take next lane R.

(2) Follow to end & take green track down to road.

[Sorry about the mud, but its a lovely old track isn't it? Distract yourself with the views of the Hillmorton radio masts and Ashlawn Water Tower.]

(3) Go ahead, cross M45 plus 100yds & take 2nd of 2 gates L.

(4) Cross diagonally to where fence meets hedge & take stile. Keep same line & take R of 2 gates.

(5) Follow hedge on your L 200yds to mark post L. Bear R & cross canal bridge. [Oxford Canal]

(6) Go ahead & take gate under power line. Keep same line (to Water Tower on skyline) & take gate.

[The sinuous ditch is the old line of the canal before straightening.]

(7) Go with hedge on your R to gate. DON'T TAKE IT. Put your BACK to gate, go ahead to L side of farm & take gate.

(8) Follow track to road. Go L (over M45 & canal), round 1st L bend & up to 2nd.

(9) Ignore track R & next gate & take L gate. Go with hedge on your R, round R bend & on 15yds.

(10) Turn L & cross field to take gate. Keep same line by hedge (via gates) & join green track to track junction by farm.

****
Route (B)
(10a) Go L appx .5 mile to Barby & start.
****
Route (A)

(11) Take track ahead, then with hedge on your R & take gate to track. Follow to road junction.

[On this high and breezy point is a squalid and rotting old mill, a sinister spidery radio mast and a potty sized water tower. All very odd]

(12) Take Kilsby road .5 mile (pass double row of oaks L) to take concrete stile L.

(13) Go diagonally L & cross midhedge stile 70yds from road. Keep same line to R field corner & take stile. ◀

(14) Go ahead, bearing R to far R field corner. Pass R thro gappy hedge, & with hedge on your L down to last power pole.

(15) Take stile & bridge L. Follow path to road, then thro churchyard to start. ●

Bilton & Northampton Lane

WHERE?
Map reference SP 484737. Bilton is a western suburb of Rugby on the A4071.

PARK/START
Use the car park opposite Lloyds Bank, otherwise, park very carefully in streets nearby. Start from Bilton Green in front of the George Inn.

HOW FAR?/FACILITIES
Route (A) 4.25 miles, Route (B) 3.7 miles or Route (C) 3 miles. All three start on Route (A). The walking is mostly on field paths, tracks or lanes. Only a very short section of track is likely to be dirty in wet weather. There is a pub at the start.

MAPS
Landranger sheet 140, Pathfinder SO 47/57 (956).

BILTON & THE WALKS
It is mentioned in the Domesday Book, but to someone driving out of Rugby, Bilton now seems little more than a green and some shops on a bend. Certainly it has been engulfed by suburbs, but if you stop and look it still has some of the character of a distinct and pleasant village.

On the green are some stocks last used in 1866 and the stump of a cross. The George overlooking the green was a coaching inn with smithy behind. The oldest building is the half timbered Old Granny's Pie Shop which used to be thatched. The picture of Granny shows an unfathomable old girl, somewhere between the Mona Lisa and Alfred of MAD magazine.

St Marks church was built of red sandstone in the Decorated style in 1350 and restored in 1873. It has deeply impressed some visitors with its "grand but quiet beauty". Some of the windows have fragments of medieval glass.

Here we have three rewarding walks with a common start. You walk a short distance along Northampton Lane, once the main road between Coventry and Northampton, and now a hippo's paradise. Walk (A) finishes along a splendid avenue of lime trees. These are the common variety, a hybrid of small and large leaved limes which for a period after the last Ice Age were England's commonest tree. They have been planted and pruned for their beauty, colour and scent, but do not leave your car to catch their sticky deposits.

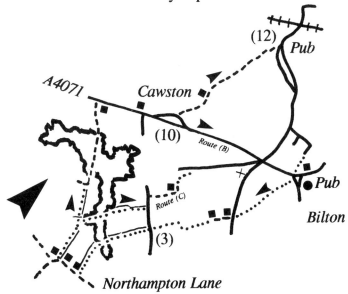

Routes (A),(B) & (C)

(1) From Bilton Green take path L of Old Granny's Pie Shop to road. Take path opposite (thro allotments, past sports field) to road.

(2) Enter Scots Close opposite & follow track past house. Follow fenced path (via bends) to lane.

(3) Take gate opposite & with hedge on your R (via gate) to spinney.

[See how many trees and plants you can spot round the silted pond. There is alder, elder, holly, young oaks, hazel, birch, hawthorn and brambles before you start looking seriously. These little wet areas encourage variety and act as a pool of wildlife in rather hard managed farming areas.]

(4) Go with hedge on your R to gate & track.
[Northampton Lane]

(5) Go R, pass farm & cottages R, to L bend. Take path R before last house. ◀

[Look out for the cottage with the County's bear and ragged staff plaque, dated 1922.]

(6) Follow via 2 gates, then with hedge on your R (via gate) to field corner with wooden fence.

****
Route (C)

(6a) Cross fence & follow woodland path. Pass paths L & R & take stile into field corner.

(6b) Go with wood then fence on your L (via dog leg) to gate & lane. Go L 100yds & take track R.

(6c) Follow to end & take gateway to field. Go L & round field edge to take corner stile.

(6d) Enter avenue of trees & go R to end. Go L to main road, then R back to start. ●

*Routes (A) & (B)
continue*

▲

(7) From field corner with wooden fence, go L 25 paces & take stile R. Go with hedge on your R to track.

(8) Go ahead thro spinney & farm to A4071.

[As you enter the spinney note the old octopus like hazel on the left. It must have been last coppiced many years ago. This is a fine little wood of sky tall trees; ash, beech, Scots pine, larch and spruce. Some are covered to the top with ivy. Lower down are big spreading yews and laurel.]

(9) Go R appx .4 mile (past lane R) to just opposite layby L. ◢

****
▲ *Route (B)*

(9a) Follow road ahead .8 mile to start. ●

****
▲ *Route (A)*

(10) Enter layby & go 200yds to take 2nd gate L.

(11) Follow track (via gates) appx .7 mile to junction with lane.

(12) Go R to main road. Go R .3 mile (down dip & up past school) & take Nelson Way L.

(13) Follow to post box & take Queensferry Close R. Exit via path L & back to start. ●

Bilton Cross (Rtd)

Timber frame, brick & thatch at Flecknoe

(33)

Braunston & Flecknoe

WHERE?
Map reference SP 543663. Braunston is about 7 miles south-west of Rugby by the A45 to Daventry.

PARK/START
Street parking in the centre of Braunston. Start from the Wheatsheaf Inn.

HOW FAR?/FACILITIES
Route (A) 5 miles, Route (B) 6.25 miles. The walking is mainly on pasture with some lane. In wet weather when the ground is soft you may find (A) heavy going. Pubs in Braunston and Flecknoe.

You can combine this walk with Ashby St Ledgers & Braunston to give walks of 11.5 (Route A) or 13 miles (Route B). Just do the AStL & B walk before or after these, starting at AStL & B walk paragraph (5) followed by (1) to (4).

MAPS
Landranger map 151 & 2, Pathfinder SP 46/56 (977).

BRAUNSTON & CANALS
Braunston sits on a ridge and the spire of All Saints church is a landmark for miles. The village is pleasant enough but no more than a long main street; what people come to see is the canal down below.

This section of the Grand Union Canal opened in 1796 after the navvies had overcome problems of moving sand in the 2,042 yard Braunston Tunnel. It is the longest canal in the country, linking Birmingham with London. Just west of the village the GU meets the Oxford Canal going north to Rugby.

There are simple and seemly brick buildings with the functional beauty of the canal builders. Look for the fine iron side bridge and the 18th century dry dock. The basin is the stub end of the original route of the Oxford canal which you meet on several walks. We have shown it on the map. There are rows of narrowboats and cruisers, two boatyards, three canalside pubs and six locks. All are first class for "gongoozling", or idle watching.

All Saints church is built from attractive sandstone and ironstone with an engaging crocket encrusted spire, but the interior seems pointy and narrow. In the spacious churchyard are a cluster of amazingly tall yew trees. Yews have been known to live up to 1,500 years but are usually quite squat. Compare these with the tallest in the UK at Midhurst, Sussex which is 82 feet. Nearby is a prim and sailess brick windmill wearing a metal cap, which disturbingly resembles a hairnet.

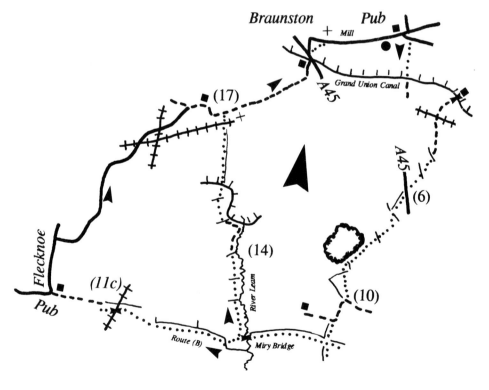

✳
Routes (A) & (B)

(1) From Wheatsheaf Inn, cross road to L of roundabout & take footpath between houses 29 & 30

(2) Follow via 2 iron gates, then down midfield & take bottom gate. Cross canal.

(3) Go L on towpath past No. 1 Lock, & appx .3 mile to Admiral Nelson pub L.

(4) Go up R onto bridge & take green track. Cross old railway & on 2 fields.

[The railway ran between Daventry and Long Itchington where it met the Rugby – Leamington line. Have a look behind at Braunston spread out on the ridge, with the edge of Dunchurch on the horizon.]

(5) Take gateway, pass brick shed on your R & go with fence/hedge on your R to A45.

(6) Take gate opposite & keep same line with hedge on your R, to take field corner gate.
◀

(7) Keep same line, making for skyline mast ahead. Take hedge gap & go ahead by wood edge to field end.

(8) Take path into valley & cross bridge. Bear half L across field corner & take gate.

(9) Sight R end of power line ahead & head for last dip between poles. (If fieldpath obstructed try R edge.) Take hedge gap to farm road.

(10) Go R (via cattle grid) appx 200 yds to R bend. Go ahead with hedge on your R appx 150 yds, & take gateway.

(11) Go R with hedge on your R appx .4 miles, & down to valley bottom bridge. Miry Bridge over the infant River Leam] ▶

****
◀ *Route (B)*

(11a) From small brick bridge go ahead to tree clump on crest & take gate beneath.

(11b) Go with hedge on your R & keep same line appx .4 mile. When hedge ends, bear R to far R field corner & cross rail bridge. ▶

▰

(11c) Go with hedge on your R appx 250 yds & take gate R. Take track to house & lane.

(11d) Take lane R appx 500 yds to junction & turn R. Follow appx 1.25 miles (over 2 railways & past farm) to church.

[The east-west railway is one you crossed near the canal. The other was the Great Central Railway's main line via Aylesbury to London, Marylebone. See note in Onley & the Rainsbrook. The ponds before the farm are part of the old route of the Oxford Canal.]

NEXT para (17)
****

▲ Route (A)

(12) Go R with line of stream. After appx 100yds ignore meanders & go ahead to take small gate.

(13) Keep same line with hedge on your R (ignore meanders), & take steel farm gate to track.◀

[See Braunston church and mill on the horizon.]

◀ (14) Follow field edge track, round L corner by steep bank to its L end, & take gate R.

(15) Go ahead via next gate, then bear a little R & on to next. Go with hedge on your R & under rail bridge.

(16) Go on to lane by church & turn R.

▲Route (B) rejoins

(17) Follow track appx .6 miles to A45.

[The troughs and hummocks in the fields on the left are all that remain of the of Wolfhampcote and Braunstonbury. See the other Braunston walk. The villagers were driven out in the "enclosures" of the 18th Century.]

(18) Go a few yards L & join canal towpath. Go R .6 mile to No. 1 Lock, then cross canal back to start.●

Braunston, Sawbridge & Wolfhampcote

WHERE?
Map reference SP 537662. Braunston is about 7 miles south-west of Rugby by the A45 to Daventry.

PARK/START
Start from the War Memorial in Braunston churchyard. Park nearby.

HOW FAR?/FACILITIES
About 4 miles of level walking on tracks and field paths. Pub at the start.

You can link this walk to Ashby St Ledger & Braunston. Go to the Wheatsheaf Inn at the opposite end of the main street from the church, and start with AStL & B walk para (5).

MAPS
Landranger sheet 151 & 152, Pathfinder SP 46/56 (977).

WOLFHAMPCOTE, THE CHURCH AND THE CANALS.
As you walk from Braunston on a track you cross the county boundary from Northants into Warwickshire. On the right are several grassy mounds, all that remains of the villages of Braunstonebury and Wolfhampcote whose people were turned out in the enclosures of the 18th century. Also right and just before the church is a big mound. Aerial photographs show it was the manor house, and hexagonal in plan. However the most interesting survival is the church.

St Peter's is small and squat in yellow local ironstone and pink sandstone and has outlived its village by five centuries. It is now redundant and used only occasionally for worship. The earliest stone work in the bottom part of the tower is from the 13th century, the nave is 14th century and the clerestory roof 15th. If you go inside (get a key from the cottage just beyond the church) the east window at first looks 15th century too, but the whole chancel is a Victorian gothic job. The roof is a cheerfully elaborated king post truss structure, there is a Norman font, a hexagonal inlaid pulpit and ten of the benches/pews are from the 14th and 15th centuries. The tower houses two bells, a great one cast in 1450 and a small one in 1780. We are accustomed to old stone, but survival of a near living thing with a voice, like a bell, is somehow more dramatic. Poor St Peter's has suffered vandalism so that its windows are now plastic rather than glass, and the graves are tumbled in a sea of tall grass, but we would bet on it outlasting us.

At several points you meet the Grand Union and the Oxford Canals. From Braunston Junction the GU runs south-east and north, the Oxford runs west. When the Oxford reaches Napton Junction it heads south, and a resumed GU runs north west, so the section from Braunston to Napton is joint.

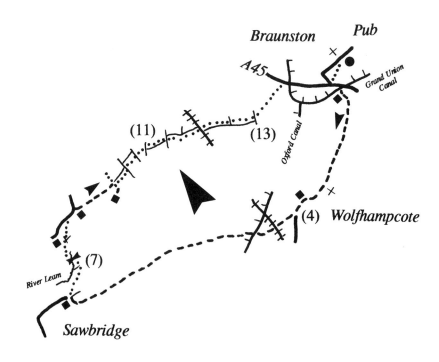

(1) From churchyard war memorial, take tarmac footpath opposite & go down to A45.

(2) Go L 50yds (cross bridge) & take track R. Pass fork R & on to church.

(3) Go on 400yds (track becomes lane) past farm R to fork. [NB Ponds L.]

(4) Go ahead under power lines & cross railway bridge to canal. ◀

[The railway cutting seems very wide. In fact it was the double track main line of the Great Central Railway between Rugby and London. For details see Onley & the Rainsbrook.

The Oxford Canal lies in a cutting, deep, leafy and silent. Look right to Braunston church and you can see the cut on an embankment. This was built in the 1820's and shortened the canal by many miles. Before this and other work was done, boatmen would travel all day and still hear Braunston's church bells.]

(5) Follow track ahead ◀ *appx 1.25 miles to farm.*

(6) Where track bends L between buildings, take DOUBLE GATE ahead, then gate R to field. Go ahead, but bear L to meet river [Leam] *& follow to ash tree & gate.*

(7) Go ahead & cross bridge & weir, then with river on your R to take stile.

(8) Go ahead to gate in farm buildings. DON'T TAKE IT. Cross fence R, then next fence. Pass corner of barn, then of house, to stile & road.

(9) Go R to lodge on bend & take small white gate. Go with fence on your R 400yds to take CORNER gate (R of 2).

(10) Go with hedge on your L to hedge corner. Keep same line ahead (via small gate) & take midhedge gate.

▶

(11) Go with hedge on your R & take gate, then hedge on your L, curving L under railway [GCR again.] (via 2 gates) to field.

(12) Go R to corner & take small gate L. Go with hedge on your R appx 500yds to field corner & take double gate.

(13) NB slate roofed house L of church. Head for gate 50yds L of it, & lane.

(14) Join canal & go R. Cross twin bridges to next bridge, & exit to A45.

[That was the Grand Union, with the Oxford to the right.]

(15) Cross & go R 50yds to take gate R back to start.

●

Through the mist - St John the Baptist, Brinklow.
The photo was taken from the top of the Motte,
which is a worthwhile diversion after Para (1) of
the Brinklow & Stretton walk.

Brinklow &
Stretton Under Fosse

WHERE?
Map reference SP 437796. Brinklow is on the A4027 about 7
miles east of Coventry.

PARK/START
Street parking near the church, which is your starting point.

HOW FAR?/FACILITIES
About 6 miles with canal, field path and some small lanes.
Pub at the start and in Stretton.

MAPS
Landranger 140, Pathfinders SP 47/57 (956) & 48/58 (936).

BRINKLOW, THE FOSSE AND THE WALK
Brinklow is a long straggling village with a few thatched and
some half timbered houses, but most are nineteenth century
red brick. Clearly, it is on the road to somewhere, and the
map shows that it was on the Romans' mighty Fosse Way
between Exeter and Lincoln. The main local monument is
the Motte, an Iron Age fort which was used by the Romans
to guard the Fosse, and later by the Normans.

The church of St John the Baptist is of grey and pink
sandstone mixed with the district's creamy limestone. Like
so many churches in the area, the stone has not weathered
well and it looks battered and worn. Mostly of the late
Perpendicular style with lofty pointed arches, the chancel
is Victorian. The darkly fantastic roof with elaborate
hammer beams out-gothics the gothic. Note how the floor
slopes upward to the chancel. The east window is riotously
colourful and proudly complicated in the Victorian manner.
Some windows have 15th century glass roundels of birds.

On the walk you will meet some white waymarks showing
Warwickshire's bear and ragged staff. This is the Centenary
Way, a 100 mile route created to mark the centenary of the
County Council. From Kingsbury Water Park in the north
where it leaves the Heart of England Way, the Centenary
Way curves east to visit many historic or attractive places
before striking west again to rejoin the Heart of England
Way at Upper Quinton, near the Gloucestershire border.

The walk follows the Oxford Canal for a short distance.
This ruler straight section is not the most appealing part
of the Oxford, though there is a handsome iron bridge
with grooves worn by towing ropes.

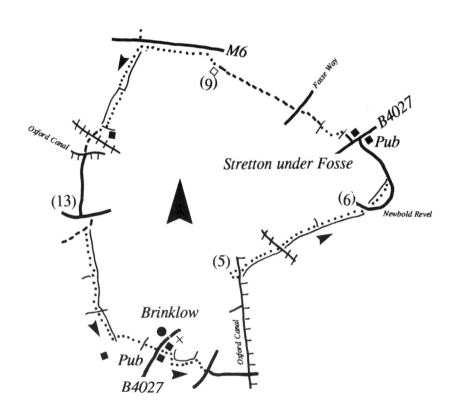

✳

(1) Face church & go R 150yds to Raven pub & take Town Gate L. Follow path & cross stile.

[The steps ahead lead onto the Motte & Bailey which are worth a visit.]

(2) Take stile R, & go with ditch on your L to take field corner stile. Go with hedge on your R to its end. Bear half R to stile under trees, and road.

[These lively green contours are all man made. The Motte is Norman, and the ridge and furrow medieaval.]

(3) Take road ahead 400yds to bridge & join towpath.

(4) Go L under bridge & .6 mile (over iron bridge, under power lines) PLUS 170 paces to take path L.

(5) Go down to stream & under canal. Go with BROOK ON YOUR R .75 mile;
 - via bends & bridge to field
 - under railway
 - thro iron kissing gate to drive of Newbold Revel.

◀

[This is the Smite Brook, once the main source of water for Brinklow and nearby villages. The big house is a college for training Prison Officers.]

◀(6) Take gate opposite & follow fenced path to drive. Go L to B4027 at Stretton.

(7) Go L 60yds. Take road R to end & cross stile. Bear L to join & follow L fence & take stile by gate.

[The Fosse Way runs along the ridge ahead. Many people find this direct route across the high points rather exciting.]

(8) Follow grass track to road. Take track opposite appx .6 mile, down dip, & up to hilltop barn.

(9) Pass barn on your L to bottom R field corner (just R of pylons) by M6, & cross plank bridge.

(10) Follow fenced track by M6 .3 mile to gate & track. [Centenary Way]

▶

(11) Go L on field edge track with hedge on your L 400yds. Take gate L, then with hedge on your R up to farm & take gate.

(12) Go ahead via gate & cross railway. Follow lane to road.

(13) Go L 100yds & take track R. Cross packhorse bridge & on 80yds to R bend.

(14) Cross (?bust) field corner stile AHEAD (not gate L). Go with hedge on your L (via 2 gates) to end of THIRD field.

(15) Take stile L & go a few paces to hedge corner. Cross midfield (pass smaller midfield tree on your R) to stile & track.

(16) Go R to road & L back to start.

Broadwell & Leamington Hastings

WHERE?
Map reference SP 438652. This reference is to the starting point about 7 miles south-west of Rugby, where the A426 Rugby - Southam road crosses the Grand Union Canal.

PARK/START
Park and start at the car park by the canal bridge on the Birdingbury road

HOW FAR?/FACILITIES
About 7 miles on canal towpaths, tracks and field paths, all are in fair condition with little mud. Pub at the start.

MAPS
Landranger sheet 151, Pathfinder SP 46/56 (977).

GRAND UNION CANAL & LEAMINGTON HASTINGS
This walk starts, continues and finishes with stretches of the Grand Union. It is a wide canal, meaning that the 14 foot wide locks can hold one large boat or two of the

narrowboats designed for other canals. The seven Stockton
Locks on this walk take the canal down 54'7". The GU falls
another 70 feet to Leamington and Warwick, then climbs
about 200 feet past Hatton and Knowle onto the Birmingham
plateau. The GU was the spine of the southern system and in
1932 the Government funded a huge modernisation programme.
Only then were these locks from Braunston to Birmingham
widened. The other main sign of restoration is many miles
of concrete banks.

The church of All Saints, Leamington Hastings has a yard
of spreading yew trees and was mainly built in the 13th
century from warm red sandstone. If you want to know
the details there are lots inside, if you take your reading
glasses or can handle small print. And for those with
binoculars there are heraldic designs in the west window.
The interior is lofty and wide with a flat wooden ceiling
and wooden chancel arch. Note the simple, flat carving
of the screen by the door, similar to work at other
local churches. In the south aisle is a fabulous small
organ, the pipes cheerfully and sumptuously decorated.

Although on the level and fertile fields of Warwickshire,
this walk is mainly through grassland It is a landscape
of hedges and little woods with slow rises and falls, but
there is a grandly scenic quarry.

*(1) At car park face pub &
follow towpath R. Pass 5
locks (.6 mile) & take
bridge to cross canal.*

*(2) Follow track appx
250yds to railway bridge.*

*(3) Go on a few paces to L
bend & take SMALL PATH off
to fence. PASS stile & go
L to corner. Go up to (R
side of cottage) & A426.*

*(4) Take track opposite &
pass farm R to fork. Go R.
[The quarry on the right
holds a deep blue lake in
a vast crater, with a
skyline of romantically
sculpted waste tips. It
produced limestone for
cement and a local stone
called Blue Lias.] Follow
track (thro MSF depot) to
road junction.*

(5) Go L 300yds to canal. Take towpath R .7 mile (under steel bridge) to red brick bridge.

(6) Step L onto lane & take gate opposite bridge. Go with hedge on your R & take gate.

(7) Bear L & take midhedge gate. Bear L to join hedge & follow it to field corner by brick thingy L.

[In fact it was a barn and is now a jump for horses. If you are a horse we sympathise.]

(8) Go L with hedge on your R 200yds & cross jump R. Put your BACK to jump & canter over field corner to markpost & hedge gap.

(9) Keep same line to join earth track. Go R to farm, curve L along fence & take gate R. Take gate ahead & go L to lane.

(10) Go ahead thro village (Broadwell) & round R bend, pass green iron building & Chapel, to L bend by barns.

(11) Take gated track R & round L bend to A426.

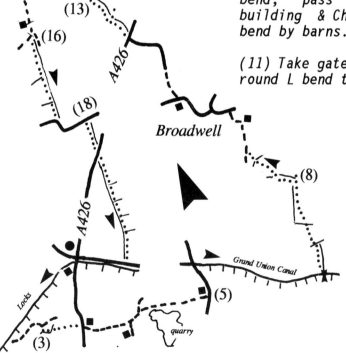

Leamington
Hastings

(13)

(16)

A426

(18)

Broadwell

(8)

A426

Grand Union Canal

Locks

(5)

(3)

quarry

(12) Take stile opposite & go ahead. Join R hedge, & follow to field corner & 2 stiles.

[This is fine throwing mud. Walkers at the back of a party can gather lumps on their walking sticks and lob it forward to hit the leader. HEALTH WARNING. Like all enjoyable activities, this is not good for you.]

(13) Take L stile, go with hedge on your R to field corner & take stile.

(14) Go ahead to join & follow R hedge, via stile, to corner stile & lane. Go L to R bend.

[The Almshouses were built in 1696 and recently restored. Note the flakey Blue Lias stone used with the more common grey-brown limestone, the alternate courses of large and flat stones, and the plaque. The church is just round the bend.]

(15) Take track L 450yds & pass barn R via gate. Go on 100yds to fork & TAKE GATE.

(16) Go L with hedge on your L (CHECK - L with hedge L) for 3 fields to lane bend.

(17) Go ahead, round L bend, & on 250yds to last power pole L.

(18) Take stile R & go with hedge on your L to A426. Take gate/stile opposite. Go with hedge on your R (via stiles) .6 mile to lane.

(19) Join towpath & go R to start. ●

(48)

Almshouses at Leamington Hastings

Indian Bean Tree in Leamington Hastings churchyard.

(49)

Clifton &
Brownsover Reservoir

WHERE?
Map reference SP 532764. A village on the B5414 about 2 miles north-east of Rugby and 1 mile west of the A5.

PARK/START
Start from the church, beside which is a car park.

HOW FAR?/FACILITIES
Route (A) 3.5 miles, Route (B) 4.4 miles. This is easy walking on field paths and firm surfaces. No real mud. Pub at Clifton.

MAPS
Landranger sheet 140, Pathfinder SP 47/57 (956).

CLIFTON AND THE WALK
Clifton clusters round a road junction; just a church, a Post Office, a pub and an antique shop. There are rows of small brick houses and it all has a certain leafy charm.

St Mary's church is basically 13th century with some 14th century extensions. It once had a spire which crashed down in a storm. The church houses a drum shaped lead casket in which lies the heart of Sir Orlando Bridgeman. In medieval times important people sometimes left bits of themselves to different churches and abbeys. Bodies were boiled in wine until nice and soft, then carved into the required portions. We do not know whether this can still be arranged, but if you are important you could find out. If you are not, you could start by changing your name to Orlando.

This walk combines rural grassland with urban open space. After a section on field paths Route (A) joins the Oxford Canal. Route (B) continues into the suburbs on a tour of a delightful green reserve. Like many fruits of Britain's green mental revolution, it is nature reserve, dog strollery, playground, lovers' lane and mental refreshment bar.

The canal section is also a wildlife haven. At one point the surrounding woodland is so thick that you may not realise that its lies on a huge embankment. Towards the end you meet the young River Avon, reedy and meandering.

Peer over the bridge at Para (11) & see the complex of railway lines, a reminder that Rugby was once a focus for railway companies; London & North Western, Midland and (quite late) Great Central. The embankment and arches which you meet after the canal section were the Great Central's line, now disused and converted to a walk.

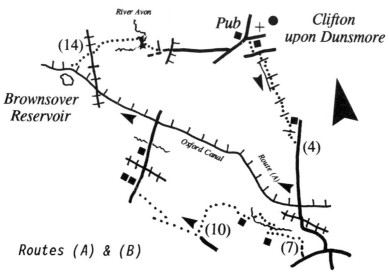

Routes (A) & (B)

(1) Opposite church is Townsend Memorial Hall. Take path on its L to road.

(2) Go L 25yds & take path by No 52 to stile & field. Go with hedge on your R & take corner stile. ◀

(3) Head for stile in opposite hedge. Keep same line towards silo, passing projecting fence corner to field corner stile & road. ▶

(51)

(4) Go R on R verge to crest of hill. CROSS to L verge & go down to canal.

****
Route (A)

(4a) Go R on towpath appx 1 mile to bridge 66.
      NEXT para (11)

****
Route (B)

(5) Go under railway (L arch) & up to T junction.

(6) Go R appx 300yds to Nos 305/7 & take tarmac path R to its end.

(7) Bear L to pass Scout hut fence corner on your R, & on to sewage works R. Path bears L, then R with bungalows L, to tarmac path.

(8) Go R over bridge, then L 100yds, then L over bridge. Go up with gardens L to end of road L.

(9) Go R on tarmac path, pass open grass area L, to sports ground. Head for nearest tower block & meet main road.

(10) Go R, cross railway & down hill, then up 100yds & join canal towpath L. DON'T GO UNDER BRIDGE.

Route (A) rejoins

(11) Follow towpath .5 mile to reservoir L. At end of wall go down L to track.

(12) Go R under canal to rough field. Look R to embankment & see BIG arch. Bear R to hedge gap & cross field to take SMALL arch.

[The humps and troughs in this path are the remains of medieval ridge and furrow farming.]

(13) Cross stile, turn R & follow path to fork. Go R over bridge & pass fork L, to T junction.

(14) Go R over bridge, then bear L to brick house & take field corner stile. Go ahead appx 450yds to T junction.

(15) Go L down Main Street to pub & church. ●

Dunchurch & Thurlaston

WHERE?
Map reference SP 485713. Dunchurch is on the A45 about
2.5 miles south of Rugby.

PARK/START
The walk starts at the centre of village. Park in one of the
nearby roads so as not to increase congestion.

HOW FAR?/FACILITIES
About 3.4 miles on field paths and a track. It is pretty
level but for one small hill, and that is down. No real mud.
Pubs in Dunchurch.

MAPS
Landranger sheet 140, Pathfinder 47/57 (956).

DUNCHURCH AND DRAYCOTE WATER
Dunchurch has always been on the road to somewhere. It
appears in the Domesday Book and stands on the old coach
road from between London and the Midlands, now the A45.
The Dun Cow has the look of one of those cosmopolitan
inns which has welcomed travellers for centuries, and
the village once had twenty seven other inns or alehouses.

The village centre has three monuments. The statue of the
nonchalant Rt Hon Lord John Douglas Montague Douglas Scott
is holding a cloak and squashed bowler hat, and seems to be
enquiring who was responsible. There also is a sandstone war
memorial and a stumpy stone cross.

The row of attractive Almshouses was built in 1693. Nearby
and more or less in period is the old School House, a fine
brick town house with stone quoins in the Queen Anne style.
Half timbered houses mix with red brick and tile, some

thatch, a building in the ubiquitous 1930's Queen Anne Telephone Exchange style and a thatched bus shelter. Yet Dunchurch is all very harmonious and hard to dislike.

The village has had a church for at least 1000 years. St Peter's was largely built in the 14th century although Norman work remains in the south and east walls of the chancel. There is an attractively battered tower in red and grey sandstone and the tower arch is impressive. The stained glass is all Victorian and Edwardian with a lot of knights and angels.

Draycote Water was built in 1964, covers 600 acres, is 5 miles in circumference and holds 5000 million gallons. Water is pumped from the River Leam and stored for use in Rugby and Leamington Spa. There is a sailing club and a trout fishery. In winter there are many gulls and different water birds, and as the greatest expanse of water for many miles it is important for bird watchers. On the south side of the lake is a Country Park and picnic site at Hensborough Hill.

✳

(1) From cross roads take Southam road 600yds, over M45 to post box, & take lane R.

(2) Go 100yds & take path L (before 1st house) to driveway.

(3) Bear R with fence, then take stile opposite to field. Go down midfield dip & take gate to track.

(4) Go L to two gates & take stile R, then with fence on your L to corner stile & wood.

[Look out over the reservoir, with anglers silently casting and boats bobbing amongst the birds. This bay is very good for birdwatching in winter.]

(5) Follow path thro wood & take stile. Join concrete track up to gate & bend of lane.

[St Edmunds church was designed by Butterfield. The squat tower, tiny wooden bellcoat, small windows and steep red tiled roof suggest some simple mystery.]

(54)

Law & order at Thurlaston

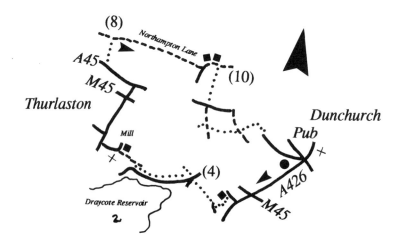

(6) Go ahead to T junction, then R down main street & over M45 to A45.

(7) Cross & go L past garage to road sign, & take hedge gap R. Go with hedge on your R to track.

(8) Go R appx .5 mile (to avoid mud keep L) to lane.

(9) Go L, round bend, & on to last house L. Go 20 paces & take hedge gap R to field.

(10) Go ahead past midfield power pole, then with bank on your L, & on track to A45.

(11) Take lane opposite to its end & take gate L.

(12) Go with hedge on your L & take corner stile. Follow fenced path round sports field to street.

(13) Go R, then L past school, & follow street to start.

St Peter's, Dunchurch - slightly battered by time

(56)

Easenhall & Newbold Revel

WHERE?
Map reference SP 466795. A hamlet about 3.5 miles north-west of Rugby on the Harborough Magna - Brinklow road.

PARK/START
Do not spoil the pretty village green by leaving cars around it. Instead park at BACK of the Golden Lion by kind permission of the landlord, Jim Austin, but not the small car park on the right of the pub. Start from here.

HOW FAR?
About 3.6 miles of field paths. The only likely mud is near the start, so if it is there you can see immediately.

MAPS
Landranger 140, Pathfinders SP 47/57 (956) and 48/58 (936).

EASENHALL AND DISTRICT
Easenhall has a very pretty village green and a handsome collection of Victorian houses in rose pink brick. The walls are built in Flemish Bond where "header" and "stretcher" bricks alternate in each course, and here the mortar joints are fine as a hair. The elaborately fretted barge boards and gable ends are all different. Work of this quality could not have been afforded by the people who lived in that type of house; they were built for people working on the estate of Newbold Revel. The Golden Lion dates from 1640 and inside still displays some of its original wattle and daub construction. They do drinks and lunches too.

A local legend is the Pailton Miser who lived in a wooden shack up Cord Lane. When he died in 1891 wads of £1 notes were found sewn into his trousers.

This is an easy walk is level countryside. You cross a railway, the Oxford Canal and pass two grand houses. One of them is Newbold Revel House which was built in red brick with sandstone dressing in 1716. It is now a college for Prison Officers.

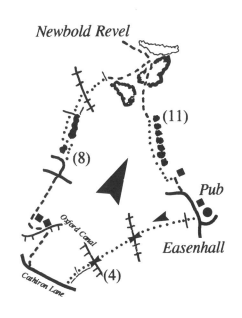

*

(1) Face Golden Lion, go R 100yds & take stile R. Follow path & cross stile.

(2) Take gate opposite. Head for L side of railway bridge.

(3) Cross railway. Go ahead midfield to green slope of canal bridge, & take stile.

[If you recognise the things on the left as tank traps, you are jolly old. These concrete roly polys were cast from dustbins to frustrate Hitler's armour.]

(4) Go with hedge on your L 2 fields to lane. Go R 400yds & take track R.

(5) Follow to cross canal & take gate. [These buildings were a pub until 1910.]

(6) Go ahead 100yds then R thro farm, & via track to road.

[The pines ahead are Corsican, which you can tell from our native Scots by the curve of the cone and the grey bark; mature Scots Pine are red. These are rather noble, but perhaps an odd choice for ornamental trees.]

(7) Take drive opposite to L bend & take kissing gate R. Cross field corner & take kissing gate. Cross green avenue & take gate.

(8) Go with hedge on your L 100yds, then L thro trees. Go R beside trees to end of block & take stile. Go ahead & cross footbridge.

[Take a look back at Town Thorns House, which is now a nursing home owned by the Motor & Allied Trades Association.]

(9) Put your back to railway & go AHEAD to gate at L end of trees. Bear R on field edge track to T junction at lake.

[This is Newbold Revel House. The lake sometimes has interesting birds. Note also the vertical axis windmill. Does it suggest a partial resolution of the current debate about wind turbines.]

(10) Go R, pass tracks R & L, leave wood & follow midfield track to end of chestnut avenue.

(11) Follow path up R side of avenue, via diversions, to gate & track by farm.

(12) Go R 40yds to cricket field. Circle round L & take gate to lane. Go R to road then L back to start. ●

Oxford Canal - almost back to nature

Frankton & Marton

WHERE?
Map reference SP 424702. A small village about 2 miles south-west from the A45 (Blue Boar junction) via the B4453.

PARK/START
Park in the village and start from St Nicholas's Church.

HOW FAR?/FACILITIES
An attractive walk of about 4 miles. The going is easy with good field paths and tracks. Pubs in both villages.

MAPS
Landranger sheet 140 and 151, Pathfinder sheets SP 47/57 (956) and 46/56 (977).

FRANKTON, MARTON & THE WALK
Frankton is a small and dreamy village lost in the fields amongst trees and ponds. Grouped in a neat square of lanes, the houses are mainly modern with a core of old ones, the Friendly Inn, the Manor House and St Nicholas's church.

The Manor was built in 1662 but the handsome doorway of Hornton stone was added in 1926. The Manor fish ponds which you pass at the start of the walk are still in use.

The church of St Nicholas is in red sandstone with a cream and blue tinged local limestone. It has a square 13th century tower but most of the rest is Victorian restoration, though distinguished Victorian by George Gilbert Scott. From the outside the church is long, low and comfortable. Inside all the glass (unusually) is plain with the glorious exception of the east window; richly colourful in a restrained design, perhaps Scott had a hand. Look at the attractive Victorian floor tiles by the entrance and in the chancel. There are four bells cast between 1607 and 1635 and the belfry has an extraordinary curved ladder, the two stiles made from the same bough.

The walk touches the neighbouring village of Marton but does not enter. However you will pass the Middleton Bridge over the River Leam, built in 1414 by John Middleton who made money in London as a mercer. Marton has its own museum of bygones and the unusually dedicated church of St Esprit.

This walk explores local fields paths, follows the River Leam for a while and climbs Windmill Hill. There are fine views of a landscape of hedges and trees which is surprisingly hilly.

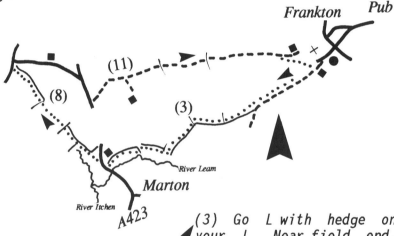

(1) Put your back to the church & take lane R. Pass 2nd fish pond to L bend, & take gate R.

(2) Go with hedge on your L to field corner & take stile. Go AHEAD to join L hedge, & follow to 2nd stile.

(3) Go L with hedge on your L. Near field end, cross to R corner & go thro line of hawthorns.

(4) Go R beside hedge along bank top & take corner stile. Pass loop of river & take stile.

(5) Go with hedge on your L & take stile L, then with hedge on your R, via 2 gates, to A423.

[The half timbered house is The Elms. In early spring the garden has a lovely show of snowdrops and aconites.]

▲

(6) To R 100yds & take gate opposite farm. Bear R to pass midfield power pole on your R, & take field end gate.

(7) Go ahead, pass bridge & bear R with hedge on your R, to its corner. Bear R & take gate L of power pole.

(8) Go AHEAD to R side of bridge, & take gate to B4455. [Fosse Way]

(9) Go R appx 100 yds & take lane R. Follow .4 mile to A423.

◄

[Stoneyford Barn which has been converted to a house. It was a smaller barn than many, so perhaps a more domestic size. Proper barns were rural

threshing factories with a big door on each side for carts and to allow the breeze to blow away husks. Turning these into enormous windows never seems quite convincing, but here the barn doors are infilled with wooden boards, which looks right.]

◄ (10) Cross & go R 250yds to take track L. Follow appx 400yds (via R bend) to sharp R bend.

(11) Take gate ahead & go with hedge on your R to take gate. Follow track to crest & take gate.

(12) Follow lane appx .4 mile to within 40yds of house L, & take stile R.

(13) Head for skyline silo & (when you see it) for L end of low stone barn. Take gate & go L back to start. ●

Hillmorton Circular

WHERE?
Map reference SP 534736. Hillmorton is a suburb of Rugby
about 2 miles east from the centre. Reach it on the A428
Northampton road.

PARK/START
Start from the War Memorial and park in a side road or layby.

HOW FAR?/FACILITIES
An easy 3.5 miles on Route (A), which can be extended using
Route (B) to 4.5. There is a canal section and tracks which
tend to be dry. The lowest part near the Rainsbrook might be
soft in wet weather. Pubs just at the start.

MAPS
Landranger sheet 140, Pathfinder SP 47/57 (956).

THE LANDSCAPE & CANAL
The main feature of this walk is the sweeping view from near
the start across a broad valley to a distant hill. Hillmorton
stands at about 400 feet and before you, the land drops into
the valley of the Rainsbrook at 300 feet. In the distance it
rises to the great whaleback of Barby Hill at nearly 500
feet. Straight ahead is Barby village with its water tower on
the skyline, and Kilsby to the left. The Rainsbrook flows
westwards to join the Leam which drains the wide plain on
the right.

The Oxford Canal runs from Oxford to Coventry. It winds
and twists around Rugby, and on this walk lies more or less
parallel with the Rainsbrook. Your map will show you that
by and large it winds along the 325 foot contour, and this
tells you that the Oxford was an early canal. It was started
in 1769 by the canal pioneer James Brindley, and concerns
about water supply and the need to control costs meant that

he tried to avoid changes of level, hence locks, cuttings and embankments. Later canals were bolder and straighter when it was realised that greater capital costs could be paid for by increased revenue from more direct and efficient routes. And as railway competition developed older canals were modernised. It was in the late 1820's that the northern Oxford Canal was straightened, cutting almost 14 miles from a 36 mile wander between Braunston and Coventry. So on this walk and several others the canal now strides over the landscape on a great embankment, leaving curly dewatered remnants.

Look at the hedge by the final path. Much of this shrubby growth is elm, some from seed but some regrowth from the stumps of mature trees which were victims of Dutch Elm Disease. Although these youngsters look optimistic and some may reach fifteen feet, generally the disease strikes as they get bigger.

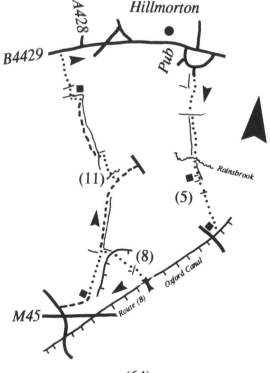

ROUTES (A) & (B)

(1) From war memorial, pass Red Lion & The Bell & take next street R, Bucknill Cresc.

(2) Follow L bend & take 2nd R (Kilworth Place) to gateway.

(3) Go ahead with fence on your R to its corner, then keep same line to midhedge tree, & take gate. Go with hedge on your R to cross stream.

[This is the Rainsbrook which marks the boundary of Warwickshire and Northamptonshire.]

(4) Go with hedge on your L via 2 gates, then keep same line & take midfence gate.

(5) Head for far R field corner & bridge, (pass shed on your R) & up bank to gate & road.

(6) Cross road, join towpath & (NOT going under bridge) follow appx .5 mile to bridge. ◀

****
◀ Route (B)

(6a) Follow canal appx .7 mile to 2nd bridge. Take stile R & up to join road.

(6b) Follow over M45 & take farm track R. Go round L bend & take gate R of house.

(6c) Go ahead parallel with hedge & bank R, to field end gate appx 100yds L of hedge etc.

NEXT para (10)
****
◀ ROUTE (A)

(7) Cross fence on near side of bridge. Go ahead & take midhedge gate.

(8) Head for skyline water tower & cross field to take gate.

[The sinuous trough here was the original line of the Oxford Canal.]

(9) Go with hedge on your R to gate R. ▶

Route (B) rejoins

(65)

(10) Take gate & go with hedge on your R, becomes track. Follow round R bend plus appx 150yds & cross stile L.

(11) Go ahead & cross bridge. Go to top L field corner & take stile.

(12) Go with hedge on your R on field edge track to farm. Go L 50yds & take stile R.

(13) Bear L & take midhedge stile. Follow hedged path to road. Go R & join A428 back to start.

The dreaming arches of Ashlawn Water Tower

Honey Hill & Winwick

WHERE?
Map reference SP 639770. The reference is to the starting point at a bend on the lane crossing Honey Hill. This is some 9 miles west-north-west of Rugby, reached via the A428 to Crick and West Haddon, then to Cold Ashby.

PARK/START
Park carefully on the verge near the above bend and start from there.

HOW FAR?/FACILITIES
A walk of about 5 miles on field paths and tracks which your map will show is down from Honey Hill and back again. No serious mud.

You can combine this walk with West Haddon & Winwick to make a circuit of 9 miles by switching to it as noted in the directions.

MAPS
Landranger sheet 140, Pathfinder SP 67/77 (957).

HONEY HILL & THE WALK
The main feature of this walk is the huge view from the 700 foot high crest of Honey Hill. There is a distant M1 to the west, the unseen Grand Union Canal, and nearby is the scar of the new A14. But the overwhelming impression is of arable fields on the level land and green pasture on the flanks of low hills, all misting and rolling away to a level horizon. The long rolling tracks that you follow through this landscape are a satisfying part of it.

We have already said a little about Winwick in the West Haddon & Winwick walk. This remote and pretty hamlet repays a visit.

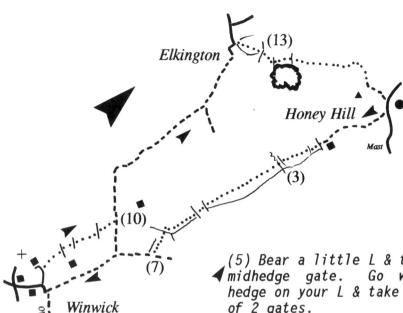

Elkington (13)

Honey Hill

Mast

(3)

(10)

(7)

Winwick

Option

(5) Bear a little L & take midhedge gate. Go with hedge on your L & take 2nd of 2 gates.

*

(1) From road bend, go towards mast & take track R. Pass house L, go down to farm, & take small gate at R end of wall.

(2) Cross small field to big one. Keep same line midfield parallel with L hedge, & take small gate.

(3) Go ahead & down bank. Bear R to waymark posts & cross stream to field.

(4) Go L to hedge, then with hedge on your L 600yds, & take small gate R of corner.◄

(6) LOOK at summit ahead, then look down R slope to 3rd tree. Head for it, passing pond on your R, then follow hedge to its corner & track.

(7) Take track R (via gate) & meet track. Go L (via gates) appx .5 mile, to gate in field corner with earth track L.

►

****
OPTION
To join or rejoin West Haddon & Winwick walk: Take track L & turn to **WH&W** para (7) point*.
****

(68)

(8) Take gate & bend R to next bend. # Take drive (Winwick Manor) appx 100yds, pass 1st iron gate R & take 2nd (small gate).

(9) Go to gap in opposite hedge 100yds L of farm & take gate. Go ahead past midfield power pole & cross midhedge bridge. Bear L towards farm (NOT GATES) & cross bridge & stiles onto track.

(10) Go L (via gate) & follow track 1.3 miles, to pass Manor L & take gate.

(11) Follow lane round R bend to next bend at Portly Banks Farm (sic). Take path R, & via iron gate to field.

(12) Put your back to gate & see 3 trees down R hedge. Go to R of lowest & take field corner gate. Go R & take gate.

(13) Take rising path curving L thro gorse to field. Keep same line, pass wood on your R & take L of 2 gates. Go with hedge on your R & take field end gate.

(14) Go ahead, curving R with L hedge, & follow green track (via gates) to start. ●

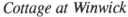

Cottage at Winwick

Newbold on Avon
& Little Lawford

WHERE?
Map reference SP 487772. Newbold is a village on the B4112
at the far north-western edge of Rugby.

PARK/START
The walk starts from the Church. There is a layby outside
but it is also a bus stop. If there is more than one car there
or on Sundays, find space down the hill by the shops.

HOW FAR?/FACILITIES
About 4 miles with field paths, tracks and a green lane and
a canal. No serious mud. Pubs at start.

MAPS
Landranger sheet 140, Pathfinder SP 47/57 (956).

NEWBOLD, CANALS, RIVERS AND AN OLD ROAD
Newbold on Avon is an urban village on the side of a big
sandstone hill. St Botolph's church on the summit stands
at about 320 feet. In warm pink and grey stone, it was built
in the 15th century on the site of a much older church.
Remains of an early tiled floor can be seen near the chancel
arch, there is an 18th century wrought iron tower screen and
masses of monuments.

The Oxford Canal passes through Newbold and heads north
towards Coventry through a fine tunnel. This was built in
the 1820's as part of a straightening exercise, and the walk
crosses the dry meandering loop of the cut off. The old line
round the hill was so extraordinary that we have shown it
on our map. The complex of canal buildings and two canal
pubs suggest that Newbold was a busy wharf.

The River Avon roams through Rugby and south of Newbold
performs a great double loop. You can see as you cross it

that it has nothing of the volume and power of the Avon south of Kenilworth, where it is joined by the River Sowe. However it used to trouble the village by regular flooding.

One section of the walk follows a long straight green track called Cathiron Lane, which runs some three and a half miles from Brinklow towards Newbold. Like most green tracks it is an old road, and like railways and canals, slightly exciting and mysterious. The beginning, the distant end and the other travellers are unknown, and you do not know what you will see. Perhaps this is the appeal of Long Distance Footpaths.

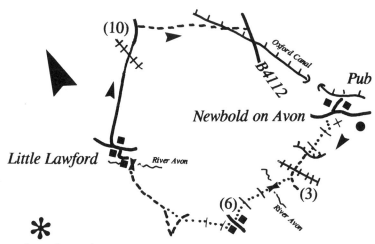

(1) Enter churchyard, pass church on your L & go 35yds to take stile R.

[The bricked up tunnel and trough shows how the old canal wandered round the hill.]

(2) Go thro avenue of oaks, take gate & cross dry canal. Keep same line & join lane. Pass under railway & take gate R. ►

[This is the railway north to Nuneaton and Tamworth. These days all the trains are painted with stripes to make them go faster, but it doesn't seem to work.]

(3) Go down & cross Avon bridge. Go up & take stile, then on to power pole with grey gizmo, & take stile.

(4) Go ahead parallel with R fence & take stile. Go L & immediately R to street & small green.

(5) Cross green, go L 30yds & take path L of No 47. Follow to end of L fence, go L a few paces & take stile.

(6) Bear L, aim between distant house (L) & barn (R), to cross bridge. Keep same line to field corner stile & track.

[This leads to Holbrook Grange which you can see on the right. To the left is St John's church, which was built in grey brick by the Caldecott family as part of the Grange estate in 1839. The interior is almost unaltered.]

(7) Take gate opposite & go ahead to stile & earth track. Go R, round L bend & cross stream.

(8) Follow track appx .4 mile, cross Avon & take gate to farm. Go L & round R bend to road.

[Little Lawford Mill is now a farm. The Hall which was demolished in the 1790's had its own fishpond, vital in winter when meat was scarce and poor. The building near the road was the stables, all that remains of the home of the Boughton-Leigh family. Note the date 1604 and the oddly shaped windows. Expert opinion thinks 1800 more likely.]

(9) Go L to junction. Take road R appx .5 mile, over railway, to iron posts R.

(10) Take track R appx .6 mile, over canal, to road.

(11) Go R, cross bridge & turn R onto towpath. Go under bridge & follow .3 mile to tunnel mouth.

(12) Go thro tunnel & on 200yds. Go R & pass Barley Mow on your L to reach road, then R to start.

Oxford Canal tunnel at Newbold on Avon

Blue brick arches stride across Ashlawn Cutting

(73)

Onley & The Rainsbrook

WHERE?/PARK & START
Map reference SP 501748. This refers to the starting point
near Rugby town centre - the Royal Oak pub on the A426
Dunchurch Road, 200 yards south of the one way system.

Street parking is possible on Dunchurch Road, but you may
prefer one of the residential streets a little way south.

HOW FAR?/FACILITIES
Route (A) is 7.5 miles and Route (B) 6.5 miles. The valley
of the Rainsbrook is low lying and often churned up by
cattle, so it can be soft in the wet.

MAPS
Landranger sheet 140, Pathfinder SP 47/57 (956).

THE WALK AND THE LANDSCAPE
This walk starts near the centre of Rugby and circles far
south into the valley of the Rainsbrook and Northamptonshire. This side of town stands at about 400 feet above sea
level and the Rainsbrook at 270 is not much less, but the
drop seems much greater and the views are wide. The
urban parts of this walk offer nothing spectacular, but
there is something pleasing in the scenes of people and
children in gardens, shopping, or playing in the parks.

Ashlawn Water Tower dominates the ridge before the
valley of the Rainsbrook like a giant on the skyline.
Built in 1934 to replace an 1852 model, it was opened by
the Mayor, and the whole Town Council and their wives
(sic) climbed all over it on iron ladders. They thought it
was a water tower, but watch the clouds and sunbeams
through those high dreaming arches. Obviously it is a
fairy castle and the little round-windowed house on top
is probably rented by a gnome.

Walks (A) and (B) both follow the vast scoop of a cutting which carried the Great Central Railway on its eccentric way through Rugby. Signboards show the Company's crest, a winged locomotive. Look closely, is it a small tank engine? The line closed in 1968 and experts question whether it should ever have opened. The Great Central was earlier known as the Manchester, Sheffield and Lincolnshire (MS&L - or "money sunk and lost"), and the name outlines its territory. Under an ambitious and enthusiastic chairman, Sir Edward Watkin, the GCR set itself to expansion and a London terminus. The other railway companies had taken the best routes (commercially and geographically) by the mid century but the GCR did not get there until 1892. Thus its line from the Midlands passed through small towns and green fields to arrived over some terrible gradients at Marylebone, the smallest, most charming and rural London terminus. In fact it was a comfortable, punctual railway with a remarkable fleet of locomotives.

Sir Edward Watkin was also chairman or director of several other railways and the Channel Tunnel Company. He was a man of great vision who died of a stroke in 1894 and did not see his dream realised of trains from Manchester to Paris via Rugby, Aylesbury, London and the Tunnel. In 1994 we have managed the Channel but the prospects of through trains to the north seem little closer.

The GCR's great Ashlawn Cutting is now a Nature Reserve managed by the Warwickshire Wildlife Trust. The mixed habitat of bankside and wet bottom areas supports a fair range of plants and creatures, whereas the habitat of the Trust is at Brandon Marsh Reserve, Brandon Lane, Coventry CV3 3GW (0203 302912).

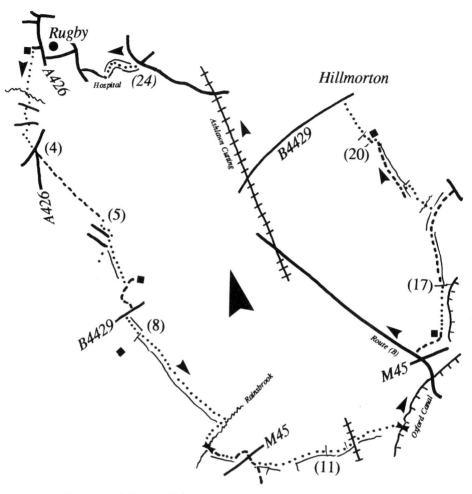

Routes (A) & (B)

(1) At Royal Oak, take East Union Street to Boys Club. Go L & down path.

(2) Join fenced path, cross Sow Brook & road. Path goes on, & is joined by service road, to T junction.

(3) Go R 50yds, then L over grass & car park. Take path between houses to A426.

(4) Take path opposite appx .3 mile to street. Take path opposite into recreation ground, & with fence on your R to its corner.

▲

(5) Take surfaced path R, cross street (Ecton Leys) & round R bend. Go on 40yds to No. 16, then L via hedge gap.

(6) Go with hedge on your R past hedge end to track. Bear R to road.

(7) Go R 70 yds & take gateway opposite. Go ahead with hedge on your L & take gate. ◀

[This sweeping view has the Vale of Evesham to the far right and just left is Barby Hill. This is an outlier of the Northamptonshire Uplands. These modest hills are part of the Jurassic belt of limestone that reaches from Bath to the Yorkshire Wolds. They also divide the headwaters of the River Leam, a tributary of the Avon, and hence the Severn, from the tributaries of the Nene which flows into the North Sea. Ten miles south the slopes of Charwelton Hill can be identified by a Post Office tower, and they are almost encircled by tributaries of the Cherwell, bound for the Thames].

(8) Keep same line with fence on your R (via gate) to valley bottom, & take gate R.

(9) Go with Rainsbrook on your L 250yds (via gate) & cross bridge L. Go ahead thro bushes, then with hedge on your R to M45.

[From the bridge have a look back to the ridge. Other people have appreciated it and you can see several big houses on the crest. The tower to the left is Bilton Grange, now a school.]

(10) Cross M45 & take gate, then on a few paces to take corner gate L. Go with hedge on your R to small pond & trees. Bear L to pass midfield plank pen on your R, then with fence on your R & take gate.

(11) Go with fence on your R, pass 2 gates & on to take gate ahead. Bear L & thro old bridge to take gate. ▶

[This is the old Great
Central line. The low
bank just before the
railway is all that
remains of sidings for a
wartime Army camp. The
prison stands on the
site.]

◢

(12) Cross electric fence
(UNHOOK & REHOOK), then
ahead to canal bridge.
Cross 2nd electric fence &
go R onto towpath.

(13) Go L under bridge &
follow to next bridge.
Pass under, take stile L,
& go up to join road.

(14) Go ahead over M45 to
farm track R.

****
◤ Route (B)

(14a) Go ahead on lane
appx .9 mile (over
Rainsbrook) to railway.

(14b) Go R .5 mile to
brick overbridge.

NEXT para (22)◀
****

◤ Route (A)

(15) Take track R & curve
L thro farm to take gate R
of house.

(16) Go ahead parallel
with hedge & bank R, to
field end gate appx 100yds
L of hedge etc.

[The hedge etc marks the
line of the Oxford Canal
before being straightened.
You can go to the gate and
look at the ditch.]

(17) Take gate & go with
hedge on your R, becomes
track. Follow round R
bend & appx 150yds to
cross stile L.

(18) Go ahead & cross
bridge. Go to top L field
corner & take stile.

(19) Go with hedge on your
R & on field edge track to
farm. Go L 50yds & take
stile R.

(20) Bear L & take
midhedge stile. Follow
hedged path to road.

(21) Go L .6 mile to
cutting & brick bridge &
go down L side to bottom.

▶

Route (B) rejoins

(78)

(22) Go under bridge & up appx .5 mile to near next overbridge.

(23) Take pebbly track L up to road. Go L .4 mile to T junction (Trevor White Drive).

(24) Take path L & round field edges into hospital. Go R past chimney & on to main (Barby) road.

(25) Go R 200 yds & take Oak St L to Dunchurch Road. Go R back to start.

Thurlaston Figure of Eight

WHERE?
Map reference SP 468711. The village lies just south of the A45 and north of Draycote Water reservoir.

PARK/START
Park in the main street. Start from the stocks.

HOW FAR?/FACILITIES
Circuit (A) is about 3 miles to the south-west and (B) some 2.7 miles to Dunchurch. Easy going, but on Route (A) a short section is convincingly muddy. Pubs on Route (B) only, at Dunchurch.

MAPS
Landranger sheet 140, Pathfinder SP 47/57 (956).

THE VILLAGE AND THE WALK
Thurlaston is a pretty village, a typical Midlands mixture of red brick with timbered and thatched houses. Trees, window boxes and tubs of flowers border the main street, a garden as much as a village. On the walk you meet a little Conservation Area where the Parish Council have planted some maples, and near the Post Office are two whitebeams. There is an old mill (now someone's house) and a small Victorian brick church of 1849 by Butterfield.

On walk (A) there are unusual views over Draycote Water. We say something about it in the walk from Dunchurch which passes closer to the water. You also pass through Draycote Meadows, a Nature Reserve of Warwickshire Wildlife Trust. This is permanent pasture which has never been ploughed or reseeded, though some basic slag was added during World War II. Such undisturbed grassland is rare and precious because over the centuries a great variety of wild flowers has grown, seeded and spread, and support many types of butterflies, grasshoppers and insects. The secret of wildflower meadows, apart from the obvious one of not spraying them with poison, is the routine of grazing and mowing. Essentially, let the flowers seed before you harvest.

Walk (B) passes through Dunchurch but we have left all our description and comment for the walk that starts from there.

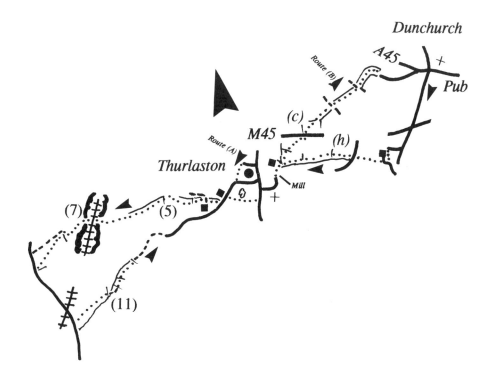

Route (A)

(1) From stocks, take Stocks Lane to its end & bear L to take stile.

(2) Go with hedge on your R to stile & lane. Go ahead 150yds to last house R & take stile R by cypress hedge.

(3) Go with hedge on your R, CROSS track, & take corner stile to field.

(4) Go with hedge on your R & take stile. Ahead see distant stile; reach it via MARK POST then power pole R.

(5) Go 500yds with HEDGE ON YOUR R (passing gaps) to end. Keep same line, pass pond on your R & take stile.

(6) Cross railway & keep same line over stream. Go ahead, rising to near edge of spinney, then bear L & curve R to fence & field. (CHECK; waymarked post is here). ◀

(7) **If crossfield path exists, follow it. If not:** Put your back to the fence & look half L. On skyline from L, see trees then BUSHES. Head for R side of them, then go R on field edge to projecting hedge corner & gap.

(8) Enter gap & cross past midfield oak to L corner gate & lane.

(9) Go L 500yds to pass under railway, plus 100yds, & take gate L.

(10) Cross field parallel with R hedge to join it, & follow to take field corner gate.

(11) Follow track to gate & field. Go with hedge on your L (via gate) to gate on track bend.

(12) Go ahead appx .6 mile (track becomes lane, past Thurlaston Grange, then between high hedges) to Broadclose Bungalow L.

(13) Take stile R & with hedge on your L, pass pool & follow hedged path to street. Go L to start. ●

****
Route (B)

(a) From stocks go down street away from M45 & take Church Lane L. Follow round L bend to end, & take gate/stile.

(b) Pass stables on your L & take stile. Go ahead & take stile. Cross field diagonally & take stile, then R & under M45.

(c) Cross field diagonally to corner stile & lane. Take stile opposite & with hedge on your L to take corner stile.

(d) Follow fenced path round sports field to street. Go R, then L past school, & follow street into Dunchurch. ◢

(e) Leave by Southam road, cross M45 & take next lane R by post box.

(f) Follow 100yds & take fenced path L to drive. Curve R with fence & take stile opposite.

(g) Bear L & down into midfield dip. Pass ruin, cross lane, & go up to take stile.

(h) Go with hedge on your L 450yds (via gates) & take L corner stile.

(i) Pass stables & take gate/stile, then kissing gate R. Go ahead via gate & lane to road. Go R to start. ●

Grand Union Canal near Norton Junction

(82)

Watford & Long Buckby

WHERE?
Map reference SP 603690. Watford is about 10 miles south-east of Rugby and just east of the A5 and M6.

PARK/START
Start from the church of St Peter & St Paul in Church Road Watford and park nearby.

HOW FAR?/FACILITIES
Route (A) is about 5.5 miles and Route (B) 7. This is gently rolling land and the walk is fairly level until a sharp final descent, giving the odd impression of being all down and no up. The arable land may be soft in wet weather.

MAPS
Landranger sheet 140 and 152. Pathfinders SP 66/76 (978) and 67/77 (957).

WATFORD, LONG BUCKBY & THE WALK
There is not much of Watford, though its name attaches to one of the best known places on the motorway system. In leafy Church Lane with a farm at one end, the impression is of rural stillness.

Outside, the church of St Peter & St Paul is in handsome mellow ironstone. The interior is tall and narrow and when we called, grey and grim. In fact it was being refurbished and the greyness arose from a coke stove used for winter heating and only just removed. The east window is a brilliant Victorian affair with lots of saints heads and some heraldry, and the floor of the nave has bold black and white chequered tiles.

Long Buckby is a straggling hilltop village of small houses in mixed style - red brick, cement rendered, ironstone and some thatched roofs. Its workaday character does not excuse the blight of overhead cables inflicted by East Midlands Electricity. There is a castle, a brick house sporting a superb wrought iron balcony, a chunky Baptist chapel and the church of St Lawrence, pleasantly encircled by lime trees.

The walk features a flowery embankment which once supported a railway bridge, a typically winding lowland stream and towards the end, a descent from a hill with views. Also near the end is an ornate railway bridge called Priest's Bridge because a priest used to hold services there for the navvies who built the line. It is a lavishly decorated minor folly adorned with an initial "H", for Lord Henley, whose park lies beyond.

(1) Put church on your L & go ahead to T junction. Go R to T junction & take hedge gap opposite.

(2) Go ahead passing midfield power pole on your R to field corner gate. DON'T TAKE IT.

(3) Turn L & go with hedge on your R to hedge corner with concrete gateposts. Take rising path 120yds, then path down R & (GREAT CARE) cross railway.

(4) Go ahead to top of bank, then R between bushes 120yds to end. Go with hedge on your R, to valley bottom & stream. ◀ ▶

****
◤ Route (B)

(4a) Go R with stream on your L .6 mile to road.

[Opposite is a converted mill, and on this side a Nature Reserve. A chart in the shelter shows the variety of habitat - ponds, hedges and grassland, with a mowing schedule.]

(4b) Go up L past Kings Head, & fork L to church.

(4c) Enter churchyard, follow tree avenue to bottom corner & take stile. ▶

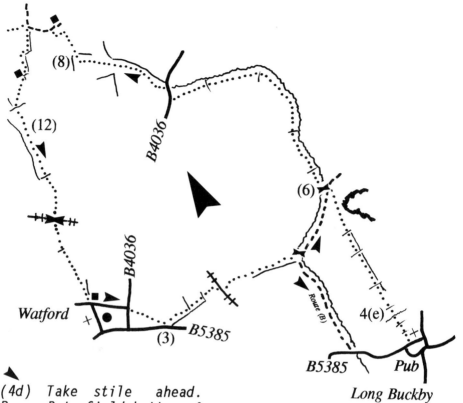

Watford   (3) B5385

B4036   (8)   (12)   B4036   (6)   Route (B)   4(e)

B5385   Pub

Long Buckby

(4d) Take stile ahead. Bear R to field bottom & cross bridge, then up to take white gate.

(4e) Go to top R field corner & take gate. Go with hedge on your R to crest, pass farm buildings & take stile.

(4f) Go ahead to pass bottom end of wood, then head for bottom field corner.

NEXT para (6)

➤

[The wood is Vanderplank's Covert, perhaps a Dutch timber merchant.]

****
Route (A)

(5) To L 60yds & cross bridge R. Go with stream on your L appx 600yds (via small gate) to field corner.

Route (B) rejoins

➤

(6) Cross field corner bridge & take gate.

(Paths in paras (6) & (7) run parallel with & not against hedge. Tractor lines may show route.)

Go R with stream & hedge on your R appx 1.3 miles;
- via small gate
- under power lines
- cross fence
- under power lines
- via gate

& on to take gate70 yds L of corner to B4036.

(7) GREAT CARE. CROSS NOW & go R 30yds to take iron gate L. Go with hedge on your R 500yds till it bends away R. Keep same line towards dip in power line, but near field end bear R & take gate.

(8) Go up thro trees towards house. After 1st (detached) brick shed, follow track L then R, to stile & track.

(9) Go L (pass drive L) to sharp R bend, & take gate ahead.

(10) Go L with fence on your L to corner gate & field. Bear R to◀

projecting hedge corner. ◀Go L, round field corner, & pass between 2 ruins to pond R.

(11) Cross field diagonally & take L of 2 gates. Go ahead past midfield power pole & take gate. Bear R to 2 small trees & join hedge.

[These are young elms, probably seeded from dead parents or grown from stumps. Since dutch elm disease few grow as high as this, but they seem healthy and if they survive it may be due to their isolated and windy position.]

(12) Go down with hedge on your R **(NB Priest's Bridge ahead)** & take bottom stile. Cross field to Priest's Bridge & pass under to field.

(13) Go ahead between 2 woods, passing close to L one. Keep same line to church & take gate (L of church & R of farm buildings) to lane.

(14) Go L & take Church Rd R to start.●

West Haddon & Winwick

WHERE?
Map reference SP 630718, a village on the A428 about 9 miles south-east of Rugby.

PARK/START
Start from the Pytchley Inn. Street parking nearby.

HOW FAR?/FACILITIES
About 4 miles on grass paths and a long track. Easy going and no serious mud. Pubs at West Haddon.

You can join this walk to Honey Hill & Winwick to make a 9 mile circular. A note appears at the appropriate place.

MAPS
Landranger map 140, Pathfinder SP 67/77 (957).

WEST HADDON, WINWICK AND THE WALK
West Haddon has a visually interesting mixture of handsome buildings. The older ones were built in the local ironstone but most are of 19th century red brick. The imposing frontages and wide main street give it more the air of a small town than a village.

The church is mainly of ironstone, and inside, austere unplastered walls enhance the stained glass. Geometrical designs in vivid colours are restrained. An elaborately carved rood screen features an awful lot of grapes.

Winwick is a tiny hamlet long lost in the fields. There is one pretty stone and thatched cottage but most houses are red brick, though one by the church has blue headers in Flemish bond to give a chequered effect. Few villages have an orange stone and shingle roofed bus shelter, war memorial and drinking fountain.

The church of St Michael and All Angels is watched over by
a tall western red cedar tree. It was first built in the 13th
century on an ancient meeting place, but what you see
is largely Victorian reconstruction. You can read the
details in the porch. Go and see the enormous memorial to
various members of the Craven family in white grey veined
marble. How would you make it "go" with the rest of the
church?

The walk leads you down through fields from West Haddon at
about 600 feet, to Winwick at 450, then back up again on a
long earth track. There are views in all directions.

✱

*(1) From Pytchley Inn go
DOWN street & take Crown
Lane R. Bear L & take
path to stile & field.*

*(2) Bear L to projecting
field corner, then with
hedge on your L to cross
field end stile.*

*(3) Go ahead midfield appx
500yds, & take stile 40yds
from bottom L field
corner.*

*(4) Bear L to pass 3 trees
& projecting fence corner
into next field. Cross
diagonally & thro gateway.*

*(5) Go ahead to white gate
& lane. Follow to village
crossroads.* ▶

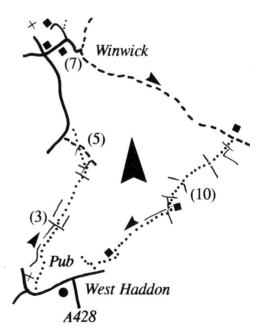

*[To see the church go
ahead. Right is Winwick
Hall, and we leave you to
work out why there are two
post boxes.]*

(6) Go R (or L if from church) past Winwick Hall to R bend.

OPTION

To join or rejoin Honey Hill & Winwick walk, turn to it, para (8) point #.

Go round R bend, then next L bend a few paces to take gate.

(7) Take track R * appx 1 mile (via gates), & up hill to take gate by white farm.

(8) Go R & take gate, then ahead & cross stile. Bear half L & take midhedge stile in opposite hedge.

(9) NB Ahead is steel barn & to R, hedge then tree clump. Head for R end of clump & cross stile.

(10) Go down & take midhedge bridge & gate. Go up to steel barn & take gate. Go on 20yds, then R over stile & bridge.

(11) Go with hedge on your R to its end, then keep same line (pass enclosure R) to sheds.

(12) Go L passing sheds on your R for 25 paces. Go R on grass path with bank on your R, to stone path.

(13) Go L to B4036, then R to start. ●

West Haddon churchyard